THE
BRITISH SEASIDE
HOLIDAY

SHIRE PUBLICATIONS

THE
BRITISH SEASIDE
HOLIDAY

KATHRYN FERRY

SHIRE PUBLICATIONS

Published in 2013 by Shire Publications Ltd, Midland House, West Way, Botley, Oxford OX2 0PH, United Kingdom. 4301 21st Street, Suite 220B, Long Island City, NY 11101, USA.

E-mail: shire@shirebooks.co.uk
www.shirebooks.co.uk

A CIP catalogue record for this book is available from the British Library.

Shire History no. 4   ·   ISBN-13: 978 0 74780 727 8

Kathryn Ferry has asserted her right under the Copyright, Designs and Patents Act, 1988, to be identified as the author of this book.

Designed by Ken Vail Graphic Design, Cambridge, UK and typeset in Bembo.
Printed in China through World Print Ltd.

13 14 15 16 17   11 10 9 8 7 6 5 4 3 2

COVER IMAGE
Detail from 'East Coast Joys No 2 - Sun-bathing', LNER poster, 1931. One of a series of six posters produced to promote rail travel to the East coast of England. The posters formed a continuous scene when placed next to each other, but each was designed so that it could also stand alone. Artwork by Tom Purvis. (Credit © NRM/Pictorial Collection / Science & Society Picture Library -- All rights reserved.)

PAGE 2 IMAGE
On the beach with a Butlin's Red Coat. After the Second World War holiday camps offered a popular accommodation option for seaside holidays.

DEDICATION
In memory of my uncle, Adam Paul James (1969–2009)

ACKNOWLEDGEMENTS
For their assistance with information and illustrations the author is grateful to Roger Billington at the Butlin's Archive, Professor Fred Gray, John Kennedy at John Hinde, Gail Durbin, Nick Evans, Zoe McLintock at Tunnels Beaches Ilfracombe, Emma Davis at Time and Tide Museum Great Yarmouth, Peter Robinson of www.thesurfingmuseum.co.uk, Simon Wills at Babbacombe Model Village, and Lawrie and Denise Davis of the Fernside Hotel. Special thanks are also due to Matthew Slocombe and all my family, and to Nick Wright and Russell Butcher at Shire.

Unless otherwise credited all images are from the author's collection.

Shire Publications is supporting the Woodland Trust, the UK's leading woodland conservation charity, by funding the dedication of trees.

CONTENTS

INTRODUCTION

THE SEASIDE HOLIDAY was a British invention which, by the mid twentieth century, had become a shared experience for millions of people. Children looked forward to the long summer days when they could build sandcastles on the beach, splash among the waves and enjoy the long-awaited treats of a donkey ride or a sugary stick of seaside rock. Their parents looked forward to the break from life's workaday routine, the opportunity to stretch out in a deck chair or wander along the pier before penning a postcard to friends that said 'Wish you were here'. Single young men and women harboured hopes of a holiday romance, showing off to a new crowd on the beach and in the dance halls. The seaside acted as the nation's pressure valve, a place of escape and amusement that had been some 200 years in the making.

In the beginning seaside holidays were a minority pastime, with the principal focus on health rather than pleasure. There was already a well-established tradition of visiting spa towns like Bath and Buxton to bathe in the revivifying mineral springs, but after eighteenth century medics publicised the results of their experiments with sea water, members of the leisured classes began to transfer their allegiance to the coast. Dr Richard Russell's Dissertation on the Use of Sea-Water (1750–2) had a huge impact, causing fashion-conscious hypochondriacs to line up at the door of his new surgery in Brighton. In 1789 King George III gave the seaside his royal seal of approval by bathing at Weymouth.

To capitalise on the new influx of visitors coastal communities provided libraries, assembly rooms and theatres to help health-tourists fill the time between early morning dips. Soon these facilities were an attraction in their own right and by the Regency period people were even starting to bathe for the fun of it. From the 1840s, new railway lines began to connect inland towns to the coast, providing cheaper travel and easy seaside access to the growing middle classes. Day excursions were run for working people but as weekends had yet to be invented and money was tight the seaside habit was by no means universal. In 1871 the right to time off was officially recognised by the Bank Holiday Act allowing many thousands of people to travel to the seaside on the first Monday in August, packing special trains and steamers to reach resorts that were overflowing with visitors.

Yet the real leisure revolution had to wait until after the Second World War, when workers finally felt the full impact of the 1938 Holidays with Pay Act. By 1947 at least eleven million wage-earners were entitled to a minimum of six days paid holiday. The great British seaside was at the peak of its popularity and the good times rolled on into the Sixties. But who went where, how did they get there and what did they do? By looking at the popular seaside holiday from the 1870s to the 1970s, this book aims to answer those questions and stir up a few happy holiday memories along the way.

Chapter One

GETTING THERE

EVERY HOLIDAY begins with a journey away from home, whether to a new place far away or a well-loved resort close at hand. In the days when travel was something out of the ordinary, this element of the holiday was as much a part of the attraction as the destination itself. There was the thrill of riding at high speed on a train and, with noses pressed to the carriage windows, the joy of catching that first glimpse of the sea. Or the excitement of packing up the family's first car for a trip to the beach at a time when even sitting in traffic jams was a novel part of the experience. Each advance in transport – from road to rail and back again – brought the seaside within reach of more and more people, changing the nature of the British coastline and transforming it from an exclusive destination to one that everybody could enjoy.

Seaside visitors in the eighteenth and early nineteenth century travelled by means of the original horse power, a form of transport that was slow and expensive. Thanks to patronage by the Prince Regent, builder of Brighton's extravagant Royal Pavilion, the London to Brighton road underwent such improvements that it became the best in the kingdom, yet the average journey time by horse-drawn coach was still six hours. This made the day trip an impossibility, so visitors were drawn only from among those rich enough to stay overnight. The arrival of the railway in 1841 changed that. The journey was cut to a mere two hours and special excursion fares were offered for working people. Within the space of twenty years visitor numbers had increased so much that arrivals on a single day – 132,000 on Easter Monday, 1862 – exceeded the *annual* total of 117,000 in 1835.

It is hard to overestimate how important rail travel was in the history of seaside holidays. Trains were the most popular mode of holiday transport from the 1840s to the 1940s. The first decade of Queen Victoria's reign was characterised by the frenzied speculation of 'railway mania'. Great Yarmouth got its rail link in 1844, Scarborough in 1845, Blackpool in 1846 and Torquay in 1848. By the 1880s every major resort had at least one station and many eventually had multiple stops operated by different railway companies. The London, Chatham and Dover Railway gave Ramsgate its second station in 1863, sending trains steaming through cliff tunnels to emerge right next to the beach. Miles of previously inaccessible coastline were transfigured by the railway, which had the power to turn small fishing villages into busy seaside towns. Engineers tested their skill laying iron pathways along the sea's edge, among the most scenic of which were the Furness Railway Company's route from Barrow to Whitehaven and the east coast stretch from Whitby to Scarborough, which provided magnificent views of Robin Hood's Bay. In south Devon, Isambard Kingdom Brunel's section of railway from Dawlish to Brixham snaked in and out of tunnels cut through red seaside cliffs to make one of the most exhilarating lines in the country.

OPPOSITE
Railways transformed the seaside and made travel exciting. In this 1930s poster two children eagerly look out of the window onto the beach at Hornsea, East Yorkshire, where they will soon be using their buckets and spades. (National Railway Museum / Science & Society Picture Library)

The London, Chatham and Dover Railway opened its station near Ramsgate sands in 1863. A tunnel was cut through the cliffs so that trains could emerge right next to the beach. Note the wooden chairs and benches that were used before deckchairs.

By the early twentieth century the railway system was approaching the peak of its dominance. The few resorts, concentrated in the West Country, that still lacked a connection got branch lines in this period including Padstow in 1899 and Lyme Regis in 1903. Well-established resorts were connected with far away cities by express services that ran north to south. Holidaymakers from Halifax in West Yorkshire could board a non-stop service to Ilfracombe in North Devon and from 1910 the service that came to be known as the 'Pines Express' began running direct from Manchester to Bournemouth, the Dorset resort famed for its pine-scented chines. Rail travel and holiday resorts had become so inextricably linked that the art posters which decorated station hoardings with attractive beach scenes in the

1920s and 1930s now stand as iconic representation of their time. Trains were no longer the only option for travelling to the coast, yet the number of passengers continued to rise as the general population increased and more people were able to enjoy the seaside habit. According to one estimate, holiday traffic at the end of the 1930s was three times that seen a decade earlier and the system was close to breaking point on some summer Saturdays.

The railway journey remained a key part of the adventure, requiring study of the timetables and meticulous planning. Luggage, once carefully packed, could be sent in advance to the chosen seaside destination, waiting there to be reunited with its owners when the day of the journey finally came. Most trains were still pulled by

In the 1930s luxurious Pullman services like the 'Bournemouth Belle' took holiday passengers to the south coast.

steam locomotives but electrification began in the 1930s, with the London to Brighton route being one of the first to benefit. From 1934 to 1972 the Southern Railway's 'Brighton Belle' sped seaward, an all-Pullman luxury electric express. The steam train 'Bournemouth Belle' also became a daily service after 1936, travelling direct from London Waterloo with the brown- and cream-liveried carriages of the

Happy holidaymakers arriving at Great Yarmouth by train in 1955. The accessibility of many resorts was seriously affected by the Beeching cuts of the mid 1960s. (Archant Norfolk)

Pullman Company offering a first-class steward service to all passengers. At the more popular end of the market third-class excursionists were as overcrowded as ever, without even the luxury of sufficient lavatory facilities. The squash, however, on the record-breaking last Saturday of July 1945, when the pent-up longings of a war-weary public saw 102,889 passengers arrive at Blackpool by train, is barely imaginable. After this high point came a temporary heyday that was followed, in the 1950s, by the steady desertion of holidaymakers for

other modes of transport. From 1951–5 the proportion of holiday journeys made by train fell from 47 per cent to 37 per cent. A decade later the swingeing cuts recommended by Dr Beeching's report on branch line closures hastened the transfer of holidaymakers from rail to road.

Paddle steamers operated around the coast, carrying thousands of passengers from city ports to the end of seaside piers. The boats seen here at Rothesay linked Glasgow with Scotland's west coast resorts.

Throughout the period of rail dominance and even before, there had been a well-used alternative in the shape of the paddle steamer. Boats had helped Margate to early popularity in the eighteenth century, as grain hoys unloading their cargo at the London docks would then return to Kent laden with passengers. The first steam packets were introduced on this route in 1815 and their descendants conveyed many thousands of people from Tower Bridge and Tilbury until 1956, when the Margate service was finally terminated. In the early nineteenth century resorts from Norfolk to Dorset got scheduled boat services from London, with routes rapidly established in other parts of the country too. Steamers criss-crossed the Bristol Channel, connecting holidaymakers from Bristol and urban South Wales with destinations in Somerset and North Devon. At Liverpool, trippers boarded boats bound for New Brighton, North Wales and the Isle of Man. Steamers heading down the River Clyde took holidaymakers from Glasgow to Scottish resorts including Dunoon, Rothesay and Largs.

Holidaymakers arriving by sea were always less numerous than those carried by rail, though their numbers were certainly significant. The journey might be longer but there was more scope for comradeship on a steamer; passengers could walk about the boat, they drank and laughed, sang and danced. Victorian manufacturers were already offering their customers incentive schemes and a boat trip up the Thames was one such lure directed at housewives in the summer of 1892, when the makers of Venus Soap and Watson's Matchless Cleanser promised a free return passage to Margate or Ramsgate on submission of ninety wrappers. The Great War brought services to a halt as steamers were requisitioned, cutting off destinations like Douglas (Isle of Mann), which saw its visitor numbers reduced to a tenth of the pre-war figure. But holidaymakers returned after that war and the next, with the thunderous turning of paddle wheels still reverberating around the British coast well into the 1950s.

On land and sea the impact of steam-powered transport was profound but not everyone was grateful for the new influx of seaside visitors. Class distinctions that were ingrained in Victorian society applied equally at the seaside and tensions emerged as a new type of person began to visit resorts that had previously enjoyed a very select patronage. Some resorts managed to cater for both markets as at Scarborough, where geography separated the well-to-do in the South Bay from those considered their social inferiors in the North Bay. Other popular resorts developed upmarket neighbours, the hallmark of which was quiet restraint: for Brighton there was Hove, Margate had Cliftonville, Lytham St Annes was more refined than Blackpool, and Southend had Westcliffe. Each kept itself consciously free of amusements that were likely to attract excursionists. Fashionable resorts with expensive hotels such as Cromer, North Berwick, Bournemouth and Eastbourne maintained their air of sophistication and their privileged clientele by doing the same. Among the servant-keeping classes there were also people who defied the vast rail network and went looking for places beyond its reach, their choice of Clovelly in Devon or Seaview on the Isle of Wight making a clear statement about their financial ability to escape the masses.

The growing middle section of society, able to display its new affluence through conspicuous consumption, was the mainstay of the Victorian and Edwardian seaside, keeping accommodation full throughout the season. Destinations mattered to these people too; a fact acknowledged by claims in 1895 that middle-class visitors heading for Margate hid their luggage labels and prevaricated about their holiday destination because of the resort's reputation for rowdy day trippers. Seaside towns were shaped by the status of their core visitors and holiday patterns that became established as a result of Victorian rail links persisted until after the Second World War thanks, in no small part, to holidaymakers' strong sense of loyalty. Working people from the East Midlands overwhelmingly opted for Skegness or Mablethorpe; from the West Midlands they favoured the resorts of North Wales such as Rhyl and Llandudno. Blackpool and Morecambe catered for

Cycling to the seaside was popular because of the extra freedom it offered, a benefit particularly stressed for women in this advertisement of 1919.

We are seeing the sights at Bognor

Motorbikes were a cheaper alternative to cars in the inter-war period. This couple are on their way to Bognor in the days before compulsory crash helmets.

the Lancashire cotton towns. Residents of the Welsh valleys picked Porthcawl or Barry Island; Bristolians went to Weston-super-Mare. Scarborough and Whitby drew crowds from Yorkshire's urban heartland, while nearby Bridlington got the rather long-winded nickname of 'Leeds-plus-Hull-cum-Sheffield Super Mare'. Londoners went to Southend, Margate or Brighton depending on where they lived in the city. As a result of this tendency places that were far away from the big population centres, like Devon and Cornwall, experienced little significant growth in the nineteenth century.

When travel options expanded in the twentieth century, moving away from the public and collective to more individual modes of transport, established patterns also began to shift. The first representation of a new personal freedom that was ultimately transferred to mass car ownership in the 1960s came with the bicycle. It assumed a recognisable form in the Safety Bicycle launched in 1876, though not until pneumatic tyres came onto the market in 1888 did cycling realise its mass potential. In the boom years of the mid-1890s cycling was *the* leisure sport, keenly embraced by the middle class and popular with women as well as men. Riding with friends or as part of a club, cyclists frequently chose the coast as their destination; Southend welcomed as many as 10,000 on just one weekend in 1909. Visitors to the town could also hire cycles from Mr Frederick Childs or Wright's Cycle Stores, both of which establishments gave lessons in the art of riding. The Cyclists' Touring Club became a powerful lobbyist for road improvements, realistic speed limits and better signage, all things that would eventually benefit motorists. Notwithstanding the car's inexorable spread, bicycles enjoyed a second golden age during the 1920s and 30s, when they allowed young people to travel at low cost off the beaten track. By this time there were also motorcycles. Famous names like Ariel, BSA and Triumph were already selling well and though long distances could be uncomfortable, especially for sidecar passengers, motorcycles gave many working people their first taste of independent motoring.

Open charabancs line the seafront at Brighton. Traffic congestion was already becoming a problem in the 1930s.

Many more holidaymakers were initiated into motoring in a charabanc, forerunner of the modern coach. In 1904 a Great Yarmouth newspaper noted the first of its kind in Britain, 'brought from Paris (where it was built) and tested on a trial trip to Potter Heigham'. They were used for scenic tours of the type previously provided by horse-drawn brakes, but it was not until after 1918 when the population, having become habituated to motorised transport as a necessary part of the war effort, took to the charabanc with a general enthusiasm. Colloquially known as 'charries', 'sharries' or 'chonkabonks', these vehicles were long, open cars with rows of bench seats in the body, each accessible via its own door. For inclement weather there was a hood that could be pulled over the entire coach, secured by leather straps to anchorages forward of the bonnet. Though passengers sat high above the ground to

Charabanc trips gave many people their first taste of motor transport but in the early days it was often a bumpy ride.

maximise viewing possibilities, charabancs had a reputation for bumpiness that probably owed much to the early use of solid tyres.

Like bicycles, charabancs experienced an identifiable boom period with holiday traffic surging in the years from 1920–2. A railway strike in 1919 was partly responsible for people seeking alternative travel to the coast and by August Bank Holiday the following year *The Times* was reporting 'larger crowds than ever' thanks to 'The Charabanc Vogue'. Saturday was particularly busy as 'the charabancs laden with travellers and luggage, turned out in hundreds and thronged the highways...' Charabancs were parked along every sea front in the country. By 1921 motor-coaching had already become a more organised proposition, with improvements in vehicle design and booking offices all over London to deal with the expected rush of reservations. In 1923 the bigger companies capable of running a competitive timetable of coastal services were pushing out the small firms and it was clear that the latest transport fad was here to stay. The concept of touring holidays had also arrived, with the Southwest an especially popular destination. And as charabancs were transformed into roofed coaches, passenger numbers continued to grow. By 1939 the Beach Garage and Bus Station at Weston-super-Mare was dealing with two million passengers a year. In the post-war period the example of Skegness was typical. Of visitors arriving in 1947, 17 per cent travelled by car, 16 per cent by coach or bus and 67 per cent by rail. By 1951 a quarter arrived by coach compared with just under 50 per cent by train, and four years later the three modes of transport were divided almost equally.

Ultimately it was the car that claimed the greatest share of holiday traffic, giving families control over their own timetable as well as the freedom to try new places. After the first five years of the twentieth century cars had ceased to be a head-turning novelty, though their number remained relatively small during the pre-First World War years. By August Bank Holiday 1920 there were clear signs of change; Bridlington welcomed 4,000 motor cars and over 6,000 people arrived at Scarborough by automobile. Most were hired and according to *The Times* the abnormal demand meant that 'many owners could have let their vehicles three times over.' In 1923 the first British car intended for the masses made its appearance. Rather unkindly nicknamed 'The Bedpan', the Austin Seven cost £165, still a lot of money for the average man. Yet as the traffic jams leaving Brighton and Blackpool

Coaches replaced charabancs as a convenient form of transport to the coast as well as a more comfortable vehicle for sightseeing.

Cars were a luxury in the 1920s allowing owners to tour previously remote areas like the Southwest. The manufacturers of Smith's Crisps were clearly aiming at the top of the market with this advertising brochure.

on summer Sundays demonstrated, car ownership was steadily increasing. In 1933 car registration passed the one million mark, many of those vehicles licensed for the summer months only.

Motorists increasingly used their cars to tour around a number of different destinations, many of them with personalised routes provided by officials of the new Automobile Association Touring Department. Resorts that had been the main attraction became the base for a wider exploration of the surrounding area in a way that would later become the norm for holidaymakers but was pioneering in the inter-war period. Morecambe was a favourite for discovering the Lake District. Whitby, Scarborough and Bridlington were likewise handy for the Whitby Moors and East Yorkshire, while the valleys and mountains of Wales were within easy distance of Llandudno, Colwyn Bay and Rhyl. This trend also brought problems to those beauty spots in the Southwest that felt the irony of a growing reputation for quietness that left them anything but. Large resorts were equally ill prepared for the influx of cars that continued apace after the Second World War, when inadequate parking was the key issue. In 1951 petrol rationing was lifted in time for the Whitsun

Bank Holiday and motoring organisations reported more than 4,000 cars an hour leaving Brighton and heading homewards up the A23. Over the subsequent decades, ring roads, bypasses and motorways cut journey times, helping to push the car's overall share of holiday journeys up from 27 per cent in 1951 to 70 per cent in 1972. At the same time another mode of transport that began its rise to popularity in the 1930s was having a major impact on seaside habits. The aeroplane meant that beach holidays no longer had to be on home soil.

In the 1950s visitors from London increasingly drove to the Kent coast instead of taking the train. The crowd gathered in front of these cars at Herne Bay is watching a Punch and Judy show.

BREAN SANDS

Brean Sands was one of many places that grew in popularity thanks to the post-war rise in car ownership. The unfortunate side effect was that the beach had become a car park by the end of the 1960s.

Chapter Two

EXCURSIONS AND OUTINGS

RAILWAY COMPANIES began operating special reduced fare services shortly after laying down their tracks. The package holiday pioneer Thomas Cook was one of the first to recognise the potential of moving large groups by rail, hiring a train on 5 July 1841 to transport 570 people from Leicester to a temperance meeting at Loughborough. The following year twenty-seven excursion coaches carried 2,364 excited, hymn-singing Sunday school teachers and pupils over the newly opened line from Preston to Fleetwood. As most working people of this period had only travelled as far from home as their legs would carry them, cheap railway trips were immediately popular. In 1844, so many people wanted to board the first excursion train from London to Brighton that it assumed monstrous proportions, finally pulling into the seaside station with sixty carriages pulled by six engines. Holiday expectations were quite different from our own. The opportunity to go away might only come once a year and then for just a single day. That day had to be grasped and every ounce of enjoyment wrung from it.

Unfortunately, affluent holidaymakers exhibited little desire to share their coastal retreats with the people who packed themselves into open third-class carriages, condemning 'trippers' as raucous invaders. They complained of noise and drunken behaviour, and a general disregard for the sanctity of the Sabbath. Sundays were the principal battleground, with the lines drawn between religious campaigners railing against the excursion ticket to hell and supporters of the National Sunday League, who lobbied to help working people escape from the hell-on-earth of factories and slums. The problem was that, before the Bank Holiday Act, Sundays offered the only free time available to most workers. Resorts fearful of losing their well-heeled clientele resisted the influx; Bournemouth, which got its branch line in 1870, banned Sunday trains until 1914 and did not receive scheduled steamer trips on Sundays until the end of the 1920s. Other seaside towns took a more pragmatic view, aware that the number of visitors who came on excursion trains provided a key source of income. By 1879 between 16,000 and 24,000 trippers arrived at Margate and Ramsgate by train every Sunday during the summer season.

Trippers were ultimately no different on a Sunday than any other day of the week, but it was the huge crowds that arrived on bank holidays that had the power to transform resorts. The 1871 Bank Holiday Act was promoted by Sir John Lubbock, a banker who felt the injustice of his employees' lack of free time. Though the legislation did not explicitly sanction universal holidays, the precedent quickly spread among other white-collar workers and from there to the wider population. On the first ever August Bank Holiday, London witnessed amazing scenes of overflowing railway stations and steamboat piers. The scramble for

OPPOSITE
A group photograph of people from Corsham in Wiltshire on a church outing to Weston-super-Mare in 1913.

Until the advent of mass motoring it was common for friends and workmates to spend time off together. This happy gang of Londoners is enjoying a day out at Margate in the 1940s.

transport to Southend and Margate was like nothing seen before and that was just from City workers. Until it was connected to London's East End by rail in 1889, Southend remained a relatively quiet and underdeveloped seaside town. From 1890 to 1914 it surged forward to join Blackpool and Margate as one of the most commercialised resorts in the country. At the height of the 1895 season some 40–50,000 visitors packed its promenade and on August Bank Holiday 1910 an estimated 100,000 people arrived at Southend by rail, steamer and cycle. Clacton, another Essex resort, came into being the same year as bank holidays, a speculative development planned with high-class visitors in mind. When the railway line opened in 1882, Clacton's image changed overnight and as excursionists poured in from the capital it took on the character of a brash and popular resort.

Anywhere within easy reach of an urban population felt the impact of bank holiday traffic. The jam-packed trains with standing room only, the animated buzz of conversation, sounds of squalling babies and hissing steam were all part of the experience. Even the comparatively small adjoining east coast resorts of Redcar and Coatham together played host to as many as 20,000 trippers from the Teeside industrial area in the 1890s. On August Bank Holiday 1897, close to 80,000 people travelled by train to Swansea, Mumbles and Gower from Rhondda, Brecon and Carmarthen. During the First World War excursion facilities were suspended but the number of people who flocked onto the trains after reintroduction in August 1920 proved

After bank holidays were introduced in 1871 the first Monday in August saw the largest seaside crowds of the year. Ordinary people put on their best clothes, boarded a special excursion train and went to the beach for a paddle.

The beach and esplanade at Southsea have all but disappeared beneath this Edwardian bank holiday crowd. In the left foreground are sailors from nearby Portsmouth docks.

their popularity. Despite increasing competition from charabancs, would-be passengers thronged Birmingham New Street station from midnight onwards to tussle for a place on the 1925 August Bank Holiday excursions to Blackpool.

A true 'tripper's paradise', the Northwest's largest resort was only marginally affected by bank holiday legislation. Blackpool grew because of the much older tradition of Wakes Weeks, which, though celebrated at different times in different places, were strongly embedded in the ancient church calendar of every Lancashire cotton town. Not even the mill clock's rule could induce workers to turn up during Wakes Week, so this customary time off was formalised during the nineteenth century into a week-long shutdown when the machines fell silent, the chimneys ceased belching black smoke and the polluted skies cleared. Also adopted in the textile centres of Yorkshire's West Riding and the Staffordshire pottery towns,

People opting for a day trip mostly did so to avoid the cost of staying overnight. This made it imperative to catch the last train home, however packed it was.

23

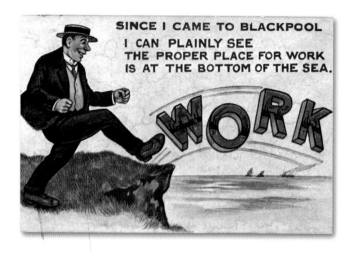

SINCE I CAME TO BLACKPOOL I CAN PLAINLY SEE THE PROPER PLACE FOR WORK IS AT THE BOTTOM OF THE SEA.

Postcards like this appealed to a seaside audience rejoicing in their liberation from work. Blackpool welcomed millions of factory workers, so here the smoking chimneys of home are being kicked into the sea.

Wakes Weeks provided Blackpool with the bulk of its holidaymakers into the 1950s. Scottish workers enjoyed similar shutdown holidays like Glasgow Fair, which gradually lengthened from a weekend to a week and saw the city empty at the end of July. The South Wales tinplate works stopped for a week at the beginning of August, releasing some 28,000 employees for their annual holiday by 1920. The communal nature of these breaks influenced the way people took their holidays, with friends, neighbours and whole streets going to the same place year after year.

Wages in the cotton belt were relatively high and there was an established culture of saving that meant textile workers experienced stay-away holidays earlier than in other industries. Employees elsewhere in the country might consider themselves lucky to get an annual staff day out, often taking the form of an expedition to the seaside and referred to as a 'holiday', albeit a brief one. Many firms were still family run, so this gesture of goodwill had its basis in paternalistic management as well as hopes for increased productivity. By the end of the nineteenth century employers were introducing their staff to far-away resorts that would otherwise have been beyond their means. In July 1884 Bournemouth was 'inundated' with more than 1,000 people from Fry's huge cocoa works in Bristol. According to a local newspaper they took to the sea on short steamer cruises, hired rowing boats and went bathing.

This timetable for the 1884 outing from Britannia Iron Works was printed on orange paper to ensure employees would not lose the details of their homeward trains. It was a long day, leaving Banbury at 4.25 a.m. and not returning until after midnight.

BRITANNIA WORKS' EXCURSION TO BOURNEMOUTH, 1884,

STOPPING AT SOUTHAMPTON,

FRIDAY, AUGUST 22, 1884.

LEAVE BANBURY... 4.25.		**LEAVE BOURNEMOUTH EAST STATION... 7.40.**	
Arrive at OXFORD ... ... 5.10.		Arrive at SOUTHAMPTON WEST 9.10.	
Nine Minutes' Stop.		Leave BISHOPSTOKE... ... 9.25.	
Arrive at BASINGSTOKE ... 6.30.		Arrive at BASINGSTOKE ... 10.11.	
Five Minutes' Stop.		*Five Minutes' Stop.*	
Arrive at BISHOPSTOKE ... 7.15.		Arrive at Oxford ... ... 11.26.	
Arrive at SOUTHAMPTON WEST 7.34.		*Nine Minutes' Stop.*	
ARRIVE at BOURNE-		Leave OXFORD ... ... 11.35.	
MOUTH EAST ... 8.50.		**ARRIVE BANBURY 12.10.**	

PASSENGERS FOR PORTSMOUTH CHANGE AT BISHOPSTOKE.

NOTE.—*The Extension Tickets are available for one week. Holders can return by any Train any day up to and including the following Friday.*

NOTE.—Passengers are requested to be at the Station ten minutes before the above times.

NOTE.—Passengers are requested *not* to leave the Train, except at the Stations marked for the Train to stop, as other Stoppages, *if any*, will only be for one minute.

Telegrams, announcing safe arrival of the Train at Bournemouth, will be despatched to Banbury as usual.

No TICKETS will be issued on the Morning of the Excursion.

PORTSMOUTH PASSENGERS.

Leave BISHOPSTOKE ... 9.5 a.m. || Return from PORTSMOUTH TOWN STATION ... ... 6.43 p.m.

The Britannia Iron Works at Banbury also chose Bournemouth for its 1884 excursion, despite a journey from Oxfordshire of nearly four and a half hours.

Works outings usually made an early start but so many people had to be conveyed to the seaside on the Bass Brewery's annual excursion that departures began in the middle of the night. Resorts like Blackpool and Scarborough ultimately got purpose-built excursion platforms, but dealing with the sheer volume of rolling stock needed for this type of away-day was a major organisational challenge. On Friday 16 June 1893, 8,000 passengers travelled from Burton-upon-Trent to Great Yarmouth on fifteen specially hired trains, the first of which left at 3.50 a.m. and returned at ten past midnight. Every ten minutes another locomotive left the station until the last at 6.10 a.m., not scheduled to return until 2.35 a.m. Such was the timetable's precision that 'It is IMPERATIVE that all persons should TRAVEL BOTH WAYS by their OWN TRAIN. Changing to other Trains, and particularly staying for LATER TRAINS, cannot be allowed, as such irregularities upset the arrangements, and seriously interfere with the comfort of the proper occupants of such Trains.' This warning was printed in a booklet that offered a guide to Great Yarmouth's attractions, together with details of all the amusements laid on for Bass employees, their wives and children. Showing their rail ticket had an 'open sesame' effect, giving free admission to the piers and entertainment venues as well as free boat trips, free bathing, free donkey rides and, just as importantly, free lavatories. Establishments that served Bass on tap and in bottles were also listed. Staff were asked to repay this effort with their best behaviour because, 'It should be an honour and great privilege to be one of the party forming, by far, the *largest Excursion* organised by a single Firm throughout the Kingdom.'

Large railway excursions continued throughout the inter-war period but charabancs offered clear benefits to smaller parties. They could make multiple pick-ups and set passengers down right on the seafront. In a charabanc everyone was seated together instead of being divided between train compartments, so the atmosphere was jolly and everyone got to know the driver, who was likely to benefit from a whip-round among his grateful passengers. Rural communities beyond the sprawling tendrils of the railway network found this new form of transport particularly useful, but the flexibility of motor travel also meant that departments within a large firm might go on separate outings. No 1 Stamping Department from Lever Bros, Port Sunlight, set out for Blackpool in August 1923 with 190 people in seven charabancs, stopping on the way for light refreshments and jazz.

A charabanc gets ready to take friends and neighbours from Laindon, Essex to Southend in 1925. (Mr and Mrs Stanley James)

A Day by the Sea
for
15,000 slum children

is provided each Summer by our Mission. The cost is small—only 2/- each : the benefit great.

600 delicate boys and girls will have a fortnight in a Country Holiday Home.

Please help to give health and happiness to these needy little ones. Gifts gratefully acknowledged by : The Rev. Percy Ineson, Superintendent,

TRAINLOADS OF HAPPINESS.

East End Mission,
Stepney Central Hall, Commercial Rd., London, E 1

Charities like the East End Mission advertised for donations in the pages of holiday guidebooks. It was thanks to them that many poor children enjoyed their first sight of the sea.

The works holiday became an institution, but it was an undreamt of luxury to those struggling to survive on the edge of poverty; for inner-city children the seaside might as well be another planet. From the 1890s, specific charitable funds set out to remedy this situation. Some had a local remit like the Newcastle-upon-Tyne Poor Children's Holiday Association and Rescue Agency, which sent 7,617 children for a full day's holiday at Tynemouth in 1895. Every summer Saturday 300 boys and girls emptied out of the city lanes and backstreets to board the steamship *Mabel*. Large meat sandwiches were provided for lunch and on arrival at Tynemouth the excited children rushed to play on the sands, enjoying buns and steaming mugs of tea before their departure for home.

The Fresh Air Fund, launched in 1892 by newspaper proprietor Arthur Pearson, provided a day out for 20,000 of London's impoverished children in its first year, extending its operation to cities throughout the country two years later. By 1909 more than two million children benefited from this phenomenally successful fundraising campaign. Charities like the Salvation Army, the East End Mission and the Shaftesbury Society and Ragged School Union, all sought donations to subsidise children's excursions, often by advertising at the front of guidebooks. By the 1930s they also ran holiday homes that allowed children and their tired mothers longer stays away from 'slumdom'. In the Depression era these trips were a lifeline; the 'Poor Children's Outing Fund' that organised an annual day out from the Stanley and Consett areas of Durham to Whitley Bay in the 1920s and '30s could easily fill a convoy of 125 buses.

In other communities it was the Sunday school trip that provided an eagerly anticipated seaside treat. Whether by train or by horse-drawn brakes, wagons and charabancs, the Sunday school outing seemed always to be blessed with glorious sunshine. Edwardian children in the small wolds village of Weaverthorpe looked forward to the day when they would assemble in front of the vicarage to board the carrier's wagon that would take them to the nearest station 5 miles away. From there the train chuffed a further 11 miles to Scarborough, to the Punch and Judy man, the wonderful works of the sand artist and the taste of penny ice creams. Perhaps there would be prayers and hymns, but this was a small price to pay for the other pleasures. In his book *Cider with Rosie*, Laurie Lee recalled the thrill of jolting along with other choirboys on the back of an open charabanc during the annual Slad outing to Weston-super-Mare. Given money to spend on treats and a souvenir for mother, the boys made straight for the pier, sucking hard on sticks of rock so as to keep a flavoursome memory until the following year. But the end of the Sunday school outing always came too soon; homeward bound, the harmonica that played brightly in the morning now lulled the exhausted children to sleep.

Music was an integral part of all excursions, with popular tunes and songs enhancing the sense of togetherness on the journey and even after arrival at the seaside.

On 1 August 1873, 300 men from the Vobster quarries in Somerset marched along Weymouth's esplanade with their wives and families behind a spirited brass band. Their holiday treat was sponsored by the quarry owners and enjoyed a musical accompaniment from five o'clock in the morning, when the merry crew set out from Vobster in twelve wagons to catch the Weymouth train at Frome. Hymns were the staple of Sunday school outings and pupils attending the pre-First World War trips from Buckfastleigh to Teignmouth processed

half a mile to the nearest railway station behind a brass band of workers drawn from the Devon town's woollen mills. Do-it-yourself music was also common, so when some of the match girls on the Bryant and May excursion missed the last train home from Southend in August 1892, they amused themselves until the early hours of the morning singing and dancing on the steps of the London Tilbury & Southend Railway station.

Someone on a charabanc trip was bound to bring a banjo or ukulele, an accordion or squeeze box, not to mention the mouth organs, swanee whistles and ever-popular lavatory paper stretched over a comb! Beer was also loaded on at the beginning of the trip to be supplemented by 'refreshment' stops on the way. When the vehicle drew into a pub there would be a piano to play, and this was such an expected element of road excursions that sheet music was advertised in coach brochures. Going to the seaside was an opportunity for an old-fashioned knees-up and alcohol consumption was not restricted to male trippers. London laundry girls of the 1930s were notorious for their Monday trips to Southend. One driver described taking a

Music was often a big part of communal outings, as can be seen in this photograph of Barrow shipbuilders on an outing to Morecambe. As well as a big bass drum there are several men playing flutes. (Gail Durbin)

A full coach park at Dreamland in the 1950s. Margate's amusement park was very popular for works outings and beanfeasts. (Bill Evans Collection)

The couples at either end of this third-class carriage are stereotypical day trippers travelling with only a picnic basket and a squeeze box. The family squashed between them have their cases packed for a stay at the seaside.

Pink rock was an inevitable souvenir of seaside excursions with the resort name running through its sugary centre. This 1920s card was sent from Mablethorpe in Lincolnshire.

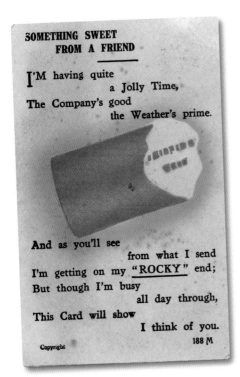

coachful of thirty-two girls on their day off along with twenty-four crates of beer: 'Well, when they got to Southend it was decided that they had perhaps better not get out, so they stopped at Billericay and ended up with whiskey and port...' Trains offered different opportunities for a shindig and the 1936 works outing of Messrs Brown and Haigh, which took five hundred staff from Wigan to Scarborough, featured a 61-foot luggage van fitted up as a dancing saloon. These lucky excursionists were also given the choice of meals in the restaurant car or light refreshments at the buffet.

Whereas a working man could always afford to sing and dance, his daily diet was limited. A good spread, including roast meats, was therefore essential to the success of a work's outing and the tradition of company-sponsored annual dinners or beanfeasts was transferred to the seaside. Some establishments specialised in this type of mass catering, and in June 1904 Messrs Atkins Bros & Co of Hastings counted among its diners the employees of Home & Colonial Stores, the Mazawattee Tea Company and a party of Berkhamsted brewers. In the early 1930s, Dreamland at Margate was the largest caterer in the country, serving more than 130,000 customers a year in eight restaurants around the amusement park. The Garden Café, Dreamland's largest restaurant, could alone seat up to 1,200 people, many of whom arrived in fleets of charabancs or streamlined coaches.

Independent excursionists were more likely to bring their own food, dispensed from bulging bags by women who had slaved the previous day to prepare it. In an age before convenience foods, station hoardings were already used to advertise one ready-made sandwich filling under the tagline 'No Summer Excursions without Bovril'. Sunday school parties also relied on mothers' baking skills, supplemented by special seaside foods such as cockles, a favourite with country children, and rock. A type of 'pulled sugar', rock was first peddled at fairgrounds before its transfer to the seaside. The addition of internal lettering first seen at Blackpool and Morecambe made it the perfect souvenir. Trippers bought tons of it every year and during the pink rock heyday of the 1950s and '60s it was *the* present expected by relatives and friends. Rationing still affected post-war outings, but 5,000 staff from Raleigh Industries Ltd of Nottingham were provided with 'an appetising box lunch' on the journey to and from Blackpool in May 1949. The biggest works outing since the war consumed a mile of sausages in 10,000 sausage rolls, 20,000 sandwiches and 10,000 cakes.

In the decades after the Second World War the sponsored away-day became surplus to requirement as people throughout society enjoyed greater affluence, paid holidays and the independent possibilities of car ownership. Mass outings and excursions now belong in the past, but thanks to them former generations of working men and women got a brief release from the grind of daily life and children got their first sight of the sea.

These factory girls sport the seaside accessory of the 1930s. The 'Kiss Me Quick' hat applied a popular catchphrase of the time to the type of headgear worn by naval ratings.

Chapter Three

BOARD AND LODGINGS

As MORE and more people visited the seaside, the demand for accommodation grew and an army of landladies rose to the challenge of providing bed and board in the streets that ran off the seafront. By the 1930s Blackpool could accommodate seven million visitors a year, Southend five and a half million, Hastings three million, Bournemouth and Southport two million, Eastbourne and Ramsgate one million each. Then as now, accommodation options varied according to budget, ranging from top-end luxury hotels to a spare bed in someone's family home. The majority of people found their niche somewhere in between and, judging from the negative stereotypes, they were willing to put up with a lot for the privilege of sleeping beside the seaside. Comic postcards made a joke out of overcrowding, rapacious landladies and unwanted insect inhabitants, themes that proved popular because of their underlying truths. Although millions of holidaymakers returned year after year, the complaints that reverberate from the past must make seaside accommodation the best example of a holiday institution we love to hate.

Eighteenth-century visitors had little choice but to rent space in existing buildings, usually fishermen's cottages. This practice was then transferred to the new Georgian terraces and Regency villas built with bay windows and balconies to capitalise on all-important sea views. Either the whole house or a suite of rooms would be taken as lodgings for the season. As long as wealthy people expected to make a protracted stay, there was little call for hotel-type accommodation. Then, stimulated by the arrival of railways, a new phase of building began which saw seafronts around the country adorned by vast and conspicuously fashionable hotels. Brighton's Grand Hotel opened in 1864 boasting 150 bedrooms, 230 marble chimney-pieces and 15 miles of wallpaper. Three years later it was overtaken by the Grand at Scarborough, a fitting palace for the self-proclaimed 'Queen of Watering Places' and the largest hotel in Europe. By the end of the nineteenth century the concept of chain hotels had emerged and the Metropole was the Hilton of its day. On the ground floor of the Folkestone Metropole, built in 1895–7, guests could enjoy a dining room, ballroom, lounge and drawing room as well as smoking, reading and billiard rooms. Yet for all these sumptuous spaces the basics were in short supply. Toilet and bathing facilities were in shared blocks, which meant that many grand Victorian hotels became redundant in the twentieth century.

The bulk of late-nineteenth-century staying visitors took rooms in the streets and terraces behind the seafront. Options broadened as demand for overnight accommodation spread, but standards of service and comfort differed markedly between family homes, apartments, boarding houses and 'private hotels'. As the price went up, so did the expectation of a certain level of behaviour. In the cheapest

OPPOSITE
Before the First World War it was common for guests to pose for souvenir photographs outside their boarding house. These people were staying at The Stanmore in Margate.

Grand hotels were built around the coast from the 1860s onward. On the cliff top outside the exclusive Hotel Metropole at Folkestone, a crowd has gathered to hear the band play.

Lees & Metropole, Folkestone.

An itemised receipt for a week's board at the Glengarry Hotel, Clacton, in summer 1952. The Grogans were charged nine shillings for 'sundries'.

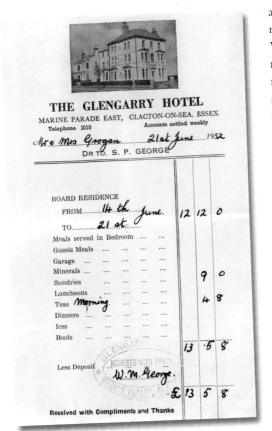

THE GLENGARRY HOTEL

MARINE PARADE EAST, CLACTON-ON-SEA, ESSEX
Telephone 1010   Accounts settled weekly

Mr & Mrs Grogan   21st June 1952
DR TO. S. P. GEORGE

BOARD RESIDENCE					
FROM 14th June			12	12	0
TO 21st					
Meals served in Bedroom	...	...			
Guests Meals	...	...	...		
Garage	...	...	...		
Minerals	...	...	...		9	0
Sundries	...	...	...			
Luncheons	...	...	...			
Teas *Morning*	...	...		4	8
Dinners	...	...	...			
Ices	...	...	...			
Boots	...	...	...			
				13	5	8
Less Deposit					
			£	13	5	8

RECEIVED WITH THANKS
W. M. George.

Received with Compliments and Thanks

accommodation the pay-off for accepting lower standards was a higher degree of freedom from house rules.

Lodging houses were the mainstay of Victorian seaside accommodation, catering to the growing middle-class market and allowing for seasonal as well as short lets. Women and children formed the majority of weekday residents, joined by Papa at weekends. From the 1890s, more working people joined the ranks of staying visitors and, as their numbers grew, the types of accommodation began to change. In Ilfracombe, for example, the 1889 listings showed 249 lodging houses, 7 boarding houses and 12 hotels. In 1902 this had become 399 apartments, 21 boarding houses and 7 hotels. Apartments were like lodgings in that guests could choose the amount of space they rented, but because the clientele was generally less well-off this ranged from the whole house to one room or even a shared bedroom, in some cases a shared bed. Prices usually included use of a communal lounge but holidaymakers bought their own food, which was then cooked by the landlady. Extra charges might be made for staples like bread, milk and potatoes, even hot water for tea making and use of the house cruet. At resorts like Blackpool, Great Yarmouth and Southend the apartment system continued to fulfil the demand for cheap accommodation throughout the 1920s and 30s.

Though they already existed in the nineteenth century, boarding houses became really popular during the inter-war years, when they began to take over from apartments.

Landladies were the butt of many seaside jokes, partly as a reaction against their role as independent businesswomen. This Edwardian gentleman had better finish his breakfast quickly or he'll see the other side of his landlady's character!

This switch to accommodation where all meals were provided at an inclusive rate was possible thanks to rising levels of disposable income and was particularly welcome to women who finally got time off from food shopping, cooking and washing up. Boarding houses ranged in size from the domestic dwelling used as a guesthouse to much larger hotel-like establishments with dining rooms where visitors traditionally ate at a large communal table. Some were single sex, catering to the high proportion

The cluttered Edwardian dining room at The Grange in Blackpool. Guests ate together at long tables decorated with aspidistras.

of young working people enjoying holidays before they settled down and the additional costs of bringing children made a seaside holiday less affordable.

Despite being widely lampooned for their petty restrictions, low-quality food, excessive charges and poor hygiene, Britain's boarding houses did very good business between the wars. On summer evenings anyone walking down the terraced streets of a seaside resort would see successive front rooms in which holidaymakers sat at their evening meal. As soon as pudding was over, the seafront would once again be packed. During the war, holidays reverted to being a rare luxury, though some landladies like Miss Settles of Scarborough tried to make the best of it. In 1940 she advertised that Blincoln House had two air-raid shelters close by and offered 'Special War Terms', promising food 'as good and plentiful as possible under rationing conditions'. Though still popular in the immediate post-war years, the boarding house name had become too linked with regimentation and was gradually dropped in favour of 'private hotel' or 'guesthouse'. As the more elite cousin of the boarding house, private hotels had been around since the 1920s. Their name was calculated to add snob value so adverts stressed better standards and the personal touch, with outdoor space and facilities like a sun lounge that hinted at modernity.

Whereas the manager of a hotel was likely to be male, apartments and boarding houses were run by women. The traditional seaside landlady was a force to be reckoned with, but history has paid her few compliments. A stereotype emerged from mid-nineteenth century accounts, which became entrenched after repetition in comedy acts and on humorous postcards. She was well past the first flush of youth, red-faced and with a figure that was large and, if not shapeless, then certainly top-heavy. She wore her hair in curlers and her feet in carpet slippers but would take no nonsense, only her guests' hard-earned cash. Her rules were the only rules that mattered and they were numerous, keeping the sexes apart, rationing bath times and dictating when visitors could and could not use their rooms. Many of these restrictions may have begun sensibly enough, aimed at regulating the behaviour of guests in a shared house run with the minimum of staff, but they soon came to be viewed as frustratingly petty. A Doncaster man who had routinely holidayed at Bridlington was driven to pastures new in 1934 because of 'irksome' strictures: 'I did not mind the aspidistras, the prehistoric family photos on the wall, the stuffed birds or the ships sailing into glass bottles... But, when, on my last visit, we could not have supper after ten o'clock and we could not have a cooked lunch on Saturday... I felt it was either time to stop at home ... or go where these mid-Victorian rules were not in vogue!'

Being a seaside landlady was hard work but for a long time it was one of the few respectable options for single women or widows in need of an income. Exploiting domestic skills by taking in visitors was also a socially acceptable way for married women to supplement their husbands' wages. Whether it was a full-time occupation or a stop-gap for a few summer weeks, the role of landlady transferred an atypical power to the mistress of the house and with it a certain resentment that helps explain the unflattering battle-axe caricatures. Between 1897 and 1911, as Blackpool's staying clientele shifted from predominantly middle class to working class, the number of landladies increased tenfold from 400 to 4,000. Of Ilfracombe's sixty-four post-First World War apartments and boarding houses, sixty-one were run by women. Holidaymakers were attracted by hometown affinities, so landladies advertised where they originally came from, often in the names they chose for their properties. Beyond this helpful familiarity, cleanliness and honesty were the key demands from a guest's point of view. If these two requirements were fulfilled then they would gladly book again for next year, with the result that many genuine friendships grew between landladies and visitors. The good landlady was treasured because popular mythology had turned her into a rare species.

In the early 1930s Hereford House, Aberystwyth, let apartments where guests brought their own food and also offered a boarding rate that included meals. The landlady came from Birmingham and mentioned the fact to attract visitors from the city.

HEREFORD HOUSE
7 Queen's Road
BOARD RESIDENCE AND APARTMENTS

C I V I L I T Y

& S E R V I C E

Situated in a residential area, 2 mins. to sea, station & tennis Electric light throughout. BOARD RESIDENCE 2 gns. from October to June.   Under the personal supervision of the Proprietress — Mrs. J. HOLYOAKE — late Birmingham

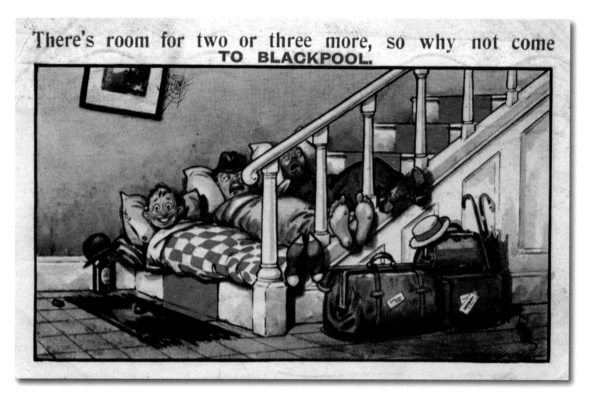

Overcrowding was a well-tested theme on comic postcards. Images like this implicitly confirmed the idea of money-grubbing landladies but also informed friends at home that the sender had chosen a popular resort.

Overcrowding was another staple of seaside humour, with comic postcards depicting people sleeping in baths and on roofs. Though scarcely credible, there are historical examples that demonstrate a high degree of desperation – as during Glasgow Fair Week in 1891, when no fewer than twenty-one people were found sharing a single room and kitchen at Rothesay. Or at Southend, where summers in the 1890s regularly saw children sent out to sleep in wooden sheds at the back of houses and where whole families were crammed into attics and basements to maximise visitor numbers. City dwellers put up with this situation partly because it was not so far removed from their own living conditions and partly because when resorts were full they were grateful for any space they could find.

Bank holiday overcrowding was particularly bad and visitors are known to have slept in bathing machines, police cells and public conveniences when the supply of sofas and temporary beds ran out. The 1926 August Bank Holiday was a record breaker, with reports from Southend of a line of 10,000 outdoor snoozers stretching some six miles along the seafront. While the lucky five hundred slept in the comfy seats of a cinema, others made do with the benches of promenade shelters or the counters of closed winkle and cockle stalls. Even in the early 1950s a good bank holiday weather forecast prompted Brighton Council to leave 2,000 deckchairs out for those who would inevitably lack accommodation. Far from easing the situation, post-war holidays with pay were looked on with dread by some resorts because people were all choosing to holiday at the same time, one-third of them on the last week of July or the first week of August. In July 1952 there were 25,000 more people than beds in Blackpool!

After wartime restrictions on catering establishments were lifted in 1950, holidaymakers temporarily forgot the poor reputation seaside food had endured since Victorian times and went back to full board with a vengeance. Breakfast was cereal, cooked breakfast or kippers, followed by toast and marmalade; lunch and dinner were both three courses: soup, fish or meat and always a proper pudding, something that went with custard. Salads were less common, acceptable for a Sunday 'high tea' but not a real dinner. At meal times the landlady would usually have help, as likely to be from husband and children as paid staff. Miss Joan Degen of Herne Bay was typical in preparing meals to a set timetable of nine o'clock, one o'clock and six o'clock each day. Her love of cooking won special acclaim from a little boy who wrote in the Visitors' Book that 'I like coming here; you can have three second helpings.'

It was much harder to satisfy guests who bought their own ingredients under the apartments system. Accusations abound of landladies creaming off the best of their guests' food, but the biggest problem was the cooking. With the best will in the world, a seaside landlady was unlikely to produce a dish that tasted the same as Mother made it for fifty-one weeks of the year. Full board removed the hassle of food shopping, but it was a more expensive option. Bed and breakfast only grew as a viable alternative after the number of cheap food outlets increased. Before 1918 women did not generally eat out, a social convention that made provision of seaside restaurants uneconomical. This situation rapidly changed after the First World War and middle-class teashops were followed by a proliferation of cafeterias and milk-bars catering for the working man and his girl. Since bed and breakfast visitors could expect to be locked out of their accommodation between ten o'clock in the morning and nine o'clock at night, they also needed cheap evening entertainments. During the 1920s and 30s, bed and breakfasters tended to be the people eating fish and chips out of newspaper in the queue for the Odeon. By the 1960s and 70s most seaside visitors had cars and did not want to cut day trips short because of mealtimes set by their landlady. Picnics were becoming more popular and in this climate many boarding houses and private hotels abandoned their lunchtime catering if not their evening meal.

If outside catering freed holidaymakers from variable food quality, technological and sanitary advances saved them from another notorious seaside complaint, bedbugs. Victorian women waged a constant war against household insects, but these creatures seem to have been particularly fond of seaside hotels and boarding houses. Trying to keep such establishments clean without the aid of modern appliances was extremely difficult and bedbugs thrived on a diet of constantly changing human flesh. Nor did they differentiate between rich and poor, as animal-lover Beatrix Potter found on a

"HAVE YOU BROUGHT YOUR FAT RATION WITH YOU ?"

A post-Second World War interpretation of an old theme. The archetypal 'Sea View' is run by a pinched-looking spinster who has suffered the privations of rationing rather more than her guest.

ABOVE
Mrs Hall was photographed in 1952 for a newspaper story on a 'day in the life of a landlady'. Here she waves goodbye to satisfied customers outside her Brittwell Guest House in Great Yarmouth.
(Archant Norfolk)

LEFT
Mr Hall serves breakfast in his waiter's jacket. Though the guesthouse was in a Victorian terrace the décor was pure Fifties.
(Archant Norfolk)

Bedbugs could make a seaside holiday very uncomfortable so sensible visitors carried their own supply of Keating's Powder and checked their bed before they got in.

stay at Torquay in 1893. Her bed at the Osbourne Hotel was infested and after an uncomfortable night with Keating's Powder in her hair she told her diary that 'it is possible to have too much Natural History in a bed.' It was no coincidence that the makers of Keating's Powder advertised their best-selling flea-killer in holiday guides. A 1913 advertisement warned, 'When packing your bag don't forget the KEATING'S POWDER. It may make the difference between an enjoyable holiday and a miserable one.'

For all its well-rehearsed faults, the seaside accommodation business was very competitive. To attract passers-by, owners of small boarding houses and guesthouses invested in external decoration that included catchy seaside names as well as brightly painted walls and floral displays. Visitors who booked in advance often relied on word of mouth or the small ads of inland newspapers, but it was also common for a family member to be sent on a cheap train to investigate and report back. From the inter-war period, official resort guides provided pages of accommodation adverts so that would-be holidaymakers could compare competing claims. It was in these years that classification by the AA and RAC began. And as expectations changed, so did the key selling points. Seafront location remained crucial; in the 1950s, Weston-super-Mare's Claremont Hotel tried to outdo rivals by claiming it was 'practically IN the Sea'. Other areas of focus included communal spaces, washing facilities and bedroom features. Edwardian hotel adverts began to refer to 'separate tables' as an indication of higher quality dining as well as electric lighting, motor garages, cycle storage, billiards, smoking rooms and bathrooms. With the Art Deco era came palm courts, cocktail bars and sun lounges, as well as central heating and beach huts for the exclusive use of residents.

En suite bathrooms were an innovation of the late twentieth century but, for many years, just to have use of an inside lavatory was a novelty for poorer holidaymakers. It was understood that facilities were shared and the daily baths

The Palace Court Hotel at Bournemouth was modern and chic, its façade wrapped in layers of 'sun-trap balconies'. Luxury venues like this epitomised the Thirties style, which smaller 'private hotels' tried to emulate.

and showers enjoyed by twenty-first-century tourists were neither a priority nor a possibility. Plumbing began to improve during the inter-war years so in the early 1930s the landlady at 37 Marine Terrace, Aberystwyth was able to offer 'H. & C. running water in some bedrooms.' Guidebooks from the 1950s show that hot and cold water was still considered an attraction, now joined by interior sprung mattresses which appeared regularly in adverts from resorts around the country.

Other amenities listed in the 1955 Brighton guide included television and wireless, fitted carpets, bedside lights, radiator in the hall, GPO telephones in all rooms and gas fires. Specific groups such as children, honeymooners and Darby and Joan Clubs were also singled out for a warm welcome by some landladies. In response to frustrations about access to places offering bed and breakfast, it was also increasingly common to see 'keys provided', 'no restrictions', or 'full use of Hotel throughout the day'.

After the immediate post-war golden days, holidaymakers began

Westaine
Guest House
45 Beach Road
(Street plan B4.)

(Sea-Front)   Tel. **6180**

Bed & Breakfast

with use of comfortable lounge with TV etc.   From **11/6** per day. ALL BEDROOMS have H. & C. running water and Interior Spring Mattresses.

Spacious dining room, sep. tables. Keys given, access to bedrooms any time of day.

★

Garages arranged.

★

Highly recommended
Resident Proprietress:
Mrs. L. H. WEST

Osborne Hotel
6 VICTORIA SQUARE

Private Tel. 1392

●

A well appointed modern Hotel facing Sea Front, Miniature Golf Course and Grand Pier. Close to Shopping Centre and All Amusements. H. and C. in all Bedrooms. Interior Sprung Mattresses. Highly Recommended. Personal Supervision. Excellent Catering

Terms from 6 to 8 guineas.
according to season.

Open all the Year round.
Commercials welcomed.

●

Proprietress:
Miss A. H. EDWARDS

moving on from traditional landlady-type accommodation. They no longer wanted to stay put on holiday when they could tour around several destinations by car. Hotels were turned into flats and scores of boarding houses were put up for sale. The number of people visiting the seaside was actually going *up* but they were visiting in different ways. Southend saw a steady fall in staying visitors after 1944 and though by the late 1970s six million people still arrived during the season, 98 per cent of them came for the day. Surviving landladies and hoteliers had to adapt or face closure. In the past, holidaymakers on a limited budget had been prepared to put up with a lot to stay beside the seaside. As the choice of accommodation options grew over the twentieth century, it was clear they no longer had to.

Two accommodation advertisements from the 1959 guide to Weston-super-Mare. Both stress hot and cold water in all bedrooms plus interior sprung mattresses. The Westaine permits all-day access with a key.

The Victorian exterior and late 1960s interior of the Fernside Private Hotel, Sandown. The family-run business stressed a lack of rules and offered a lounge with licensed bar, colour television and darts.

Chapter Four

SELF-CATERING

THE TERM 'self-catering' did not really come into popular use until the 1960s but the concept had been around for a long time. It meant the rejection of traditional seaside accommodation, freedom from the landlady's timetable, a cheaper family break and, most of all, independence. An ever-increasing proportion of holidaymakers took to the road with a tent or caravan. Holiday bungalows and chalets were another option. Then there were old train carriages and buses with the seats stripped out, forerunners of the many thousand static caravans that dot the British coastline today. This was the do-it-yourself seaside holiday and it had its roots in the late Victorian period.

Camping of itself was nothing new, but its evolution into a leisure pursuit was a development of the twentieth century. In 1901 Thomas Hiram Holding formed the world's first camping club, the Association of Cycle Campers, which would later become The Camping and Caravanning Club. Holding came up with the idea of bringing fellow enthusiasts together after a cycle camping expedition with four friends in Connemara, Ireland. From an original membership of thirteen people the club had grown to some 400,000 by the time of its centenary. This example highlights the amazing growth in camping's popularity, but Holding was by no means the only Victorian interested in sleeping under canvas. Tents were mass produced for nineteenth-century soldiers and the Boer War of 1899–1902 created a surplus. In the summer of 1900 Philip Hammond, ironmonger of Gorleston on the Norfolk coast, advertised 'Second-Hand Army Bell Tents: waterproof canvas, 40ft circumference with poles, runners, lines, mallet and bag… Suitable for bathing, cricket, tennis, lawns or camping out. Cash price 32s. 6d.' A further outcome of the Boer War was the creation of the Scout movement by its great hero Sir Robert Baden-Powell. The first scout camp took place in 1907 on Brownsea Island, near Poole in Dorset, and from this original Edwardian template generations of boys and girls discovered the joys of camping.

Thanks to the influence of health and beauty movements after the First World War, camping gradually lost its militaristic overtones. Outdoor pursuits like hiking and rambling became fashionable, while naturism took hold among the most fervent advocates of sun bathing. Youth hostels opened to provide accommodation in out-of-the-way places, but camping was the obvious accompaniment to this new trend. By the inter-war period equipment was becoming more sophisticated, with lighter-weight tents and a range of 'modern' accessories. In an article of August 1923, *Open Air: The Magazine for Lovers of Nature and Outdoor Life* suggested to readers that, 'Instead of taking the family to some crowded seaside resort, why not enjoy a healthy, jolly holiday under canvas? Family camping presents few difficulties and is an altogether delightful way in which to spend the days of freedom.' As dedicated campsites were still few and far between, the practice of negotiating space in a

OPPOSITE
Campsites in the 1960s, like this one at Seasalter in Kent, could be quite colourful places. The caravans were privately owned so came in a variety of shapes and sizes.

Bell tents were first used by the army and could be bought as surplus for camping. This Edwardian family is staying among the sand dunes at Mablethorpe.

farmer's field meant that this genuinely *was* a way of enjoying the quiet coast. *Open Air* recommended that a married couple with two young children should invest in a 'large cottage' tent which, with fly-sheet, poles in three sections, pegs, guys, proofed ground-sheet and a ground-blanket, cost £12 and was 14 pounds in weight. Bedding options consisted of woollen blankets, sleeping bags or down-filled quilts. Other necessaries included a Primus stove and enamel cups and plates. Aluminium was the new material for cooking utensils and pans, also exploited to make the handy kettle-teapot and 'a wonderfully light milk-can with a tight fitting lid' that will 'appeal strongly to the lady camper'.

This was outdoors life aimed at the car-owning end of the market, yet camping appealed across the social spectrum because it could be managed on a proverbial shoestring. By 1938 an estimated half-million people took a camping holiday of three days or more. Thousands of single young men strapped a tent on the back of their bikes and cycled off for a weekend at the seaside. They thought nothing of an 80–100-mile round trip, frequently setting out on a Friday evening after work in order to wake up to a pan of sizzling bacon and eggs fried by the beach. For families, it was the massive growth in post-war motoring that turned camping into a viable option and people who chose to fend for themselves often proved to be more adventurous in their choice of destinations. And they didn't just rely on cars; some families even made cross-country coach trips with their camping gear squashed into the seats around them. Other determined parents opted for a couple of tents, a motorcycle and a sidecar. Unable to go much above 40 miles an hour along the country roads of pre-motorway Britain, one family from Norwich took four days to travel to their holiday destination

TOP

Camping at Hayling Island in 1932. Behind the tents is a selection of old vehicles that have been converted into holiday accommodation.

BOTTOM

Increased car ownership helped to make camping more popular. To transport their luggage and camping paraphernalia home from Hayling Island, this family had to pack the inside and outside of their Morris Cowley.

A combined brochure and booking form for 1950s camping coaches. The living spaces were simple but functional.

of Sandy Bay near Exmouth in Devon. Their motorcycle journey was long, but they camped along the way and that was part of the fun.

Of course, camping had its downsides as anyone who has ever tried it will attest. Sleeping under the stars was one thing, sleeping under a torrential downpour quite another. Unreliable British weather blighted many a camping holiday, turning fields into muddy swamps and clothes into damp rags that were impossible to dry. Wildlife could also cause problems, from small but mean mosquitoes to curious cows, or worse, bullocks. Getting used to the hard ground at bedtime was usually only accomplished the day before it was time to go home. Yet for an increasing number of people the rain, the insect bites and the sleepless nights were still preferable to the iron rule of the seaside landlady. They weren't enough to put people off. Campsites grew in number and by the 1960s they were getting smarter. Many seaside resorts got municipal facilities, like the large camping ground at Sheepcote Valley near Brighton. According to an advert of 1963, 'a modern shop supplies the campers' requirements and all the conveniences of an up-to-date camp, including hot and cold shower baths available.' Tents were also getting more comfortable thanks to the invention of man-made waterproof fibres. In 1969 the film *Carry on Camping* confirmed the growing mass appeal of this type of holiday.

By this time caravanning had also captured the British imagination. In 1885 Dr William Gordon Stables designed the first purpose-built touring caravan, a 2-ton, horse-drawn, luxury 'land yacht' he called 'The Wanderer'. Travelling around the country, he inspired an upper-class band of 'gentleman gypsies' who, in 1907, founded The Caravan Club of Great Britain and Ireland. Within five years women accounted for nearly one third of the Club's 267 members. Yet caravans remained

A couple relaxing outside their caravan in the 1950s.

a distinct novelty. Early enthusiasts built their own, often resembling nothing so much as a shed on wheels. Manufacture began in earnest after the First World War when companies like Eccles of Birmingham were able to draw on the skill of ex-servicemen experienced in working with motor vehicles.

The inter-war motoring revolution spawned the romantic notion of 'motor gypsies', with most caravans custom-built to luxurious rather than practical standards. Exteriors were built to resemble country cottages with half-timbering and leaded lights; interiors came complete with electricity, wireless, plumbing and even baths. Little thought was given to the extra weight and consequent slowness when being towed. The market moved quickly, however, with middle-class members joining The Caravan Club from the 1930s and mass-production models beginning to appear at cheaper prices.

It was in the 1950s that caravans finally came into their own, with new models rolling off assembly lines to fulfil the demand from a more affluent public. Some designs, like the double-decker caravan with upstairs bedrooms, were short-lived. By contrast, the simple 11-foot box on wheels named 'Sprite' by its makers, Alperson, inspired an army of fans.

As traditional seaside accommodation fell from favour, the British love affair with caravans blossomed. By the early 1960s there were 75,000 registered touring caravans and 10,000 motor caravans, owners of the latter being welcomed into the Caravan Club fold from 1967. There were also plenty of dedicated sites, some two hundred run by the Caravan Club alone with thousands more 'certified locations' dotted around the UK. For countless families, holiday time meant towing the caravan to the seaside, setting up the awning to double the amount of internal space and dealing with the glorified bucket with a seat that lived a little distance away in the notorious 'toilet tent', known for getting swept away in a strong breeze. Mothers conjured up all manner of tin-based meals and children got used to wet weather games around the caravan's folding table. It was nice and familiar even if the chosen destination was miles away from home.

Other self-catering options relied on a fixed location, but in the case of holiday bungalows they were no less influenced by the desire for freedom and independence. Self-build plotlands became a national phenomenon during the inter-war years, with 'chalet towns' popping up from Whitsand Bay near Plymouth to Withernsea near Hull. Like camping and caravanning, this type of seaside retreat was introduced by wealthy Victorians. The first British bungalows were built in 1869–70 on the Kent coast at Westgate-on-Sea. These experimental buildings derived their name from a type of raised hut, with thatched roof and veranda, which was indigenous to Bengal and well known to ex-patriots living in India. As upper-middle-class holiday homes by the sea,

Caravanning took off after the Second World War as more manufacturers entered the market. These two models were designed with homely floral interiors, but the double-decker 'Diplomat' failed to catch on.

When the first Considerations are Comfort and Convenience — there are two alternatives...

The BEAU MANOR

The caravan for the connoisseur. Craftsman built and splendidly furnished. Air conditioned. H. & C. water, bathroom, open fire, gas lighting and cooking, and power points. Two single and one double bed. 22 ft. x 7 ft. 6 ins. - **£795**

The Peak DIPLOMAT

The superlative 22-ft. Double Decker Home. Supremely comfortable, with every modern amenity. Two upstairs bedrooms, a beautifully-equipped kitchen, H & C water, bath, gas cooker, etc. 22 ft. x 12 ft. 3 ins. of luxury living accommodation for 6 people

£1,099 . 10

See them on Stand No. 473 at the Ideal Home Exhibition.
If you cannot call, write for Illustrated Brochure.

MONTROSE Caravan Distributors Ltd

WORLD CONCESSIONAIRES FOR WILLERBY CARAVAN CO.
MAIN DISTRIBUTORS FOR ECCLES CARAVANS

Stockport Road, Cheadle, Cheshire
GATley 6179 and 5866   OPEN 7 DAYS A WEEK 9 A.M.—9 P.M.
Also HARWOOD BAR, GT. HARWOOD, near BLACKBURN and
TONMAN-STREET, MANCHESTER

Do-it-yourself holiday homes on the shingle beach at Shoreham in Sussex. This Bohemian community grew quickly after 1900 and had its own 'Bungalow Town' halt on the railway line via Brighton to London.

these buildings gave new meaning to the word 'bungalow', linking it with leisure and – thanks to artistic residents – a Bohemian lifestyle. By the end of the nineteenth century, these ideals had filtered down into the creation of makeshift holiday communities where bungalows were more likely to be based on redundant train carriages than architects' plans.

That was certainly the case at Shoreham in Sussex, where a local resident apparently noticed old railway coaches towed to the beach for use as net stores by local fishermen. With entrepreneurial foresight he marked out plots, took rent and arranged for the purchase and removal of more carriages from the London Brighton and South Coast Railway. A dozen bungalows in 1896 were transformed into a continuous line of about two hundred by 1902; within ten years it had become a 1.5-mile-long settlement dubbed 'Bungalow Town'. Shoreham proved very popular with West End theatre people who travelled down from London for weekend parties by the sea, staying in cheap but ingeniously constructed buildings. After a concrete raft was laid, old railway carriages were placed at either side to serve as bedrooms. The centre section was floored to make the main living space and a corrugated iron roof was built over the whole. There were no sewers to serve the community and people had to rely on paraffin lamps and candles, yet by 1937 there were a dozen shops and six hundred bungalows, many of them let to holidaymakers in search of the simple life.

From the outset, these cheap and cheerful shanty towns were despised by conservative Middle England, which saw only a blot on the landscape where bohemians and the poor saw a rare opportunity to shape their own environment.

Verandas were a key feature adopted from the original Indian bungalows. The Edwardian mother and daughter in this photograph sit on wicker chairs next to an elaborate example at Shoreham.

The numerous side windows in these bungalows at Sutton-on-Sea in Lincolnshire reveal how redundant railway carriages could be used as the basis for individual-looking holiday homes. A cricket match is taking place in the foreground.

Coastal property rights were uncertain, so private individuals and speculators stepped in to create democratic communities where ownership of a holiday bungalow was made all the more special by the act of building it with your own hands. At the end of the 1920s a 'simple weekend bungalow', composed of a living room, two bedrooms and a kitchen, exclusive of water, site or sanitation, could be built by one man, unaided, for less than £90. At Jaywick, near Clacton, Ford workers from Dagenham recycled packing crates to build some of the earliest bungalows on roads named after cars, like Hillman or Bentley Avenue. Other sites in Essex included Canvey Island and Point Clear, advertised in the 1930s as 'the farm by the sea'. Farther north in Lincolnshire were the Humberstone Fitties near Cleethorpes and Bohemia at Sutton-on-Sea, where imaginative use was made of circular army huts described locally as 'rusty pork pies' but known to their owners as 'O-so-cosies'. One large hut was even turned into a dance hall among the sand dunes. On the south coast pioneering Shoreham was followed by Peacehaven, Pagham, Felpham and Winchelsea Beach. Some of these holiday escapes turned into more permanent residences but others fell foul of new planning policies or wartime expediency. In 1940 Shoreham residents were given just forty-eight hours to leave before the military demolition teams arrived. Some of the original bungalows survive at Jaywick but only because their owners stood up to attempts at compulsory purchase in the 1970s.

In the days when recycling was simple common sense, railway companies also cottoned on to the value of using their old rolling stock as holiday accommodation. The London and North Eastern Railway introduced the idea of camping coaches in 1933, fitting out former passenger coaches with sleeping accommodation, living space and kitchen and then parking them in the sidings of quiet coastal and country stations.

Parties of six paid a weekly hire charge of £2 10s, and slightly larger coaches were available at £3. To help attract customers, the LNER even operated a 'Save to Travel' plan. As their name implied, the camping coaches offered a basic level of comfort and though this did not include either electricity or running water, they did come fully stocked with bedding, oil and Primus stoves, crockery, cutlery and kitchen utensils. Befriending the station master was sound advice, as he was

A 1950s photograph of the Brooklands bungalows at Jaywick, Essex. In 1929 £50 could buy 'the freehold of 1,000 square feet with a hut upon it, coloured so gaudily that you would feel you were living in a revue.'

An LMS Holiday Caravan

Camping coaches were first introduced in 1933 and were soon parked up in picturesque sidings around the country. These young women look rather smartly dressed for a week's camping, even if it is in a railway carriage rather than a tent.

51

usually a fount of local knowledge as well as keeper of the key to the station toilets! The camping coach concept proved so successful that the three other main line companies quickly followed suit and within six years they were operating 434 between them. After the war, the nationalised British Railways continued to promote camping coaches as 'a cheap and ideal holiday for the family', offering picturesque sites around the country that tended to be away from the big resorts. Scottish and Welsh coasts were well served and there were clusters in Norfolk as well as on the north-east coast above Scarborough.

In the wake of holidays with pay, demand for this sort of self-catering accommodation intensified. Wooden railway carriages that had first been used to transport Victorian excursionists were now brought out of retirement, given a cursory refurbishment and arranged in fields where they supplied the bottom end of the market. Turning up for their holiday on the Isle of Wight in 1956, one family from Fareham were shown to an old railway carriage that had been disingenuously advertised as a 'log cabin'. After three nights of sleeping on bench seats and storing their belongings in the overhead luggage racks they went home. Other old vehicles, including Edwardian buses and trams, also appeared on post-war campsites. At Bridlington, the Marton Road site offered cheap seaside holidays in converted double-decker buses, which proved especially popular with Yorkshire miners. For some visitors it was a highlight of the year, especially when relatives came and camped in neighbouring buses. There was a certain novelty in keeping food in a place that had once been used by the conductor for his tickets.

Static caravan sites often also included chalet accommodation. Judging from the number of prams in this photograph, the Welcome Stranger camp at Dawlish Warren, Devon, was popular with young families.

Others found the lack of home comforts harder to deal with. One Doncaster lady who visited in the late 1940s remembered it as an awful experience, having to sleep in big iron beds upstairs with a coal-burning stove downstairs and no curtains at the windows.

As a variation on this theme, static caravans were available to rent at many resorts by the mid-1950s. Often they were privately owned, used as a holiday home as well as being let out to provide an income against the original investment. Their numbers rapidly multiplied, with noticeable concentrations along the coastlines of Yorkshire, Lincolnshire, both sides of the Severn Estuary, North Wales, Devon and Cornwall. From a starting point of 3,000 caravans in 1950, Lincolnshire was adding another thousand every year until in the mid-1960s the number of bed spaces they provided equalled those in hotels and guesthouses. By the late 1980s caravans had seriously outstripped the seaside landlady, supplying 90 per cent of the county's holiday accommodation.

After an immediate post-war heyday it was clear that older tourist areas were losing their appeal, whereas the West Country was doing well. Road transport was the key and because of it caravan sites could colonise more remote areas. By 1969 there were 487 static caravan sites, 398 touring caravan sites and 177 campsites in Dorset, Somerset, Devon and Cornwall. Most were equipped with camp stores, bingo hall and fish and chip shop.

In many respects the static caravan was the self-catering unit *par excellence*, a bit of all its predecessors rolled into one that provided a cheap holiday with home comforts right on the coast. But it wasn't to everyone's taste and once the demand for self-catering was established a huge variety of options became available. The 1955 Bridlington guide advertised 'Furnished Holiday Flatlets – the New Idea' and by 1973 they accounted for 175 adverts. Other alternatives included chalets and bungalows, some on campsites, others like glorified beach huts right on the seafront. At the end of the 1970s, Lee Cliff Park advertised 'Modern Holiday Maisonettes' near Dawlish Warren in Devon. At Instow on the county's northern coast '"Modernised" old world cottages' could be hired and farmhouses also became increasingly popular, often shared with friends or relatives. Though it usually proved to be the cheapest form of seaside accommodation, self-catering was also about self-determination and a choice in favour of holiday independence that became increasingly pronounced throughout the twentieth century.

By 1979 there was a whole range of self-catering options as listed on the cover of this brochure.

Chapter Five

HELLO CAMPERS!

HOLIDAY CAMPS offered another option for staying at the seaside with accommodation, meals and entertainment all on one site. Billy Butlin proved himself the master of mass organisation but he was not the first to realise the potential of communal holidays. The first ever holiday camp opened on the Isle of Man in 1894, the brainchild of Mr and Mrs Cunningham. They took only young men, whereas Butlin catered for the whole family; his original camp at Skegness was fully booked before it opened in 1936. The phenomenal success of camps during the post- Second World War period owed much to the continuation of wartime team spirit combined with the wholesale implementation of holidays with pay. As self-contained communities, these holiday villages could have been built anywhere but the inter-war precedents were overwhelmingly coastal and in the popular imagination the seaside was *the* holiday place. In addition to the big name operators like Butlin, Pontin and Warner, the British coast was dotted with small independent as well as occupational camps that provided an affordable alternative to the boarding house. And so it is that knobbly knees and the cheerful refrain of 'hi-de-hi' became a part of seaside folklore.

The earliest camps tended to have charitable or philanthropic aims. Flour merchant and Sunday school superintendent Joseph Cunningham spent several years running annual summer camps for Toxteth boys' institutes before setting up on his own. His wife Elizabeth took charge of the catering and on a site overlooking the sea near Douglas they set up a business that emphasised leisure and fun over duty and tent inspections. Although eligibility was restricted to teetotal males, by the Edwardian period campers were drawn from all walks of life, middle as well as working class. By 1908 the Cunningham Camp offered plentiful cheap accommodation in rows of candle-lit bell tents, a 100-foot dining room, concert hall, bakery, barber's shop, bank and heated swimming pool. Team games and sing-songs were among the organised entertainments that fostered a feeling of community among tens of thousands of visitors every year. Cunningham's proved to be happily in tune with the inter-war craze for outdoor pursuits but adapted to the rising expectations of its campers by providing bungalows and dormitory accommodation as well as larger new 'chalet tents'. After the death of Joseph Cunningham, the camp even admitted girls who would walk up the hill from boarding houses in Douglas to attend morning and evening dances. Advertised as 'The largest, most popular holiday resort in the world', Cunningham's was requisitioned in 1939 and sold for redevelopment at the end of the Second World War.

The first of many Norfolk camps was established at Caister in 1906. In the same year its founder, John Fletcher Dodd, also formed a Great Yarmouth branch of the Independent Labour Party making clear, if his chosen name of Socialist Camp had not already, the political rather than commercial motivation.

OPPOSITE
All Butlin's holiday camps had swimming pools, which were often the focus for fun and games organised by Red Coats, as seen here at Clacton in 1948.

BELOW
Teetotallers Joseph and Elizabeth Cunningham established Britain's first holiday camp in 1894. Within ten years the camp was so successful that new facilities were added including the 100-foot dining hall seen here.

SOUVENIR ALBUM

The Cunningham Holiday Camp
DOUGLAS, ISLE OF MAN.

ABOVE RIGHT
The Cunningham Camp was only open to young men, who slept in rows of candle-lit bell tents overlooking the sea.

RIGHT
Poor boys from Manchester got regular meals and plenty of sea air thanks to the children's holiday camp at Lytham St Annes near Blackpool.

It was the first of a breed of pioneer camps that stressed co-operation. Everyone took their share in running the camp, songs around the campfire were a notable feature and the highlight of the week was a lecture on Sunday evening. Within two years of opening the local press reported on the great number of visitors and the beautiful grounds adorned with flowers and fruit trees that made Fletcher Dodd's camp 'a delectable spot'. The 'Socialist' title, however, was soon replaced by the more place specific and enduring name of Caister Holiday Camp, so that by the First World War a different clientele, drawn from the professional and business classes, was to be found enjoying the upgraded chalet accommodation that replaced the original tents.

Socially conscious holiday camps proved to be more viable when they were created as non-profit-making facilities for particular working groups. Various trade unions established camps with the first, set up by the United Co-operative Baking Society, at Roseland overlooking Rothesay Bay in Scotland, lasting from 1911 to 1974. The Coventry Co-operative Camp at Voryd near Rhyl proved hugely successful in its opening season even though accommodation in 1930 was limited to six sleeping huts, an old railway coach, an ex-army hut and a few old tents. The first Civil Service Holiday Camp opened at Corton near Lowestoft in 1924, followed six years later by a second on Hayling Island. In 1931 the National and Local Government Officers' Association took over an existing camp at Croyde Bay in Devon, then built an additional camp from scratch at Cayton Bay, south of Scarborough. None of these accommodated more than a few hundred campers but in 1939 a more ambitious

In the 1930s Corton, near Lowestoft, had two holiday camps, one of which was run for Civil Service employees. The other, at Corton Beach itself, promised 'The Holiday of your Lifetime.' After the war it became part of the Warner's chain.

occupational camp opened at Skegness, available to Derbyshire's 40,000 mineworkers and their families thanks to a welfare fund supported through a levy on every ton of coal raised by the men. During the season special trains and buses took up to 900 visitors a week to the Derbyshire Miners' Camp.

It was during the 1930s that holiday camps really began to make an impact, with new sites, large and small, opening around the country. Geographical concentrations emerged, in particular on the North Wales coast near Rhyl, which had three camps by mid decade, and the area around Great Yarmouth and Lowestoft, which gathered a remarkable cluster, including 'Pa' Potter's camp that opened at Hemsby in 1920 before moving a little way south to Hopton-on-Sea and 'Maddy' Maddieson's camp, also at Hemsby. These pioneering proprietors made their own larger-than-life characters synonymous with their camps, a tradition later taken up by men like Harry Warner, Billy Butlin and Fred Pontin. Captain Harry Warner took early retirement from the Royal Artillery in 1925 and after running a successful seaside catering business opened his first holiday camp on Hayling Island in 1931. By 1939 he had acquired a further three sites on the Isle of Wight, at Seaton in Devon and Dovercourt in Essex, where the classic television series 'Hi-De-Hi' would later be

Prestatyn Holiday Camp was a joint venture by Thomas Cook and the London Midland and Scottish Railway. Camps rarely had any architectural pretensions but, as this smart poolside building shows, Prestatyn was an exception.

filmed. His face appeared on the company's advertising and by the time of his death in 1964 Warner had amassed an empire of fourteen camps.

In a unique example of joint funding by the London, Midland and Scottish Railway and Thomas Cook and Son, the Prestatyn Holiday Camp opened on a 58-acre site in 1939. It was noteworthy for its architectural quality, with communal buildings designed in an overtly Modern style and chalets unusually planned around courts with shared washrooms. In the space of just three months a brand new settlement had risen among the sand dunes and hills of the Flintshire coast. Beyond the tall concrete arch that announced the camp's name in large Art Deco letters was the Sun Court, a large landscaped square surrounded by bright white buildings housing the dining room, ballroom and concert hall. Beside the swimming pool was a 60-foot-high observation tower with the ultimate expression of maritime references next to it in the ship-shaped Prestatyn clipper used for deck games. On opening day, 22 June 1939, Lord Stamp dubbed it the 'Everyman's Luxury Hotel' available from £3 a week for board and lodgings with 5 per cent added for tips, entertainments, sports, dancing and music. Against a backdrop that must have seemed like a movie set, visitors need spend no more, a key attraction of the holiday camp in general.

Whereas tent and caravan holidays appealed to those seeking the true outdoors life, camps promised an intermediate experience; the personal space of a private chalet together with the entertainments and catering that came from being part of a holiday community. Billy Butlin entered the market with mega-camps, accommodating far higher numbers than any of his competitors and therefore relying on a greater degree of regimentation. For holidaymakers the benefits of such a scale were to be seen in the huge range of free leisure activities as well as an entertainments programme featuring stars of cinema and radio. Indeed, Butlin himself became a star, the consummate salesman, the poor boy made good who just wanted to make his customers happy. When the 1938 Holidays with Pay Act was passed, Butlin was ready with one of his trademark catchy slogans, 'Holidays with pay: Holidays with play: A week's holiday for a week's wage'. Born in South Africa in 1899, Butlin gained experience of the travelling showman's life through his mother's West Country family and after serving with the Canadian Army in the First World War returned to England where he began a successful amusement park business. With experience of staying at a North American summer camp during his youth in Ontario, Butlin found the accommodation provided by seaside boarding houses disappointing to say the least. Thanks to the capital from his amusements business, he set out to provide what he described as 'a holiday centre for the great mass of middle-income families for whom no one seemed to be catering'.

He started at Skegness with space for 1,000 campers, specifying electricity and running water in all 600 chalets. Gambling his huge investment on the success of a newspaper advert offering holidays with three meals a day and free entertainments, he was overwhelmed by the response. Capacity was doubled the following year and continued to grow up to a peak figure of 10,000 campers per week. Clacton camp opened in 1938; Filey was due to follow two years later. Though the war got in his way, Butlin made a shrewd bargain with the armed

BUTLIN'S AYR
Aerial View of Gardens from Rope Railway

forces that saw him building military camps on a favourable post-war buy-back arrangement. His first Welsh camp at Pwhelli came into being as a result, as did that at Ayr, facing the Isle of Arran. In 1948 one in twenty British holidaymakers went to Butlin's and another 200,000 would have done so had there been room to accept their bookings. Thanks to the post-war holiday explosion, business was booming. To complete the brand's national coverage, three more camps were built at Bognor Regis in Sussex in 1960, at Minehead in Somerset two years later and lastly at Barry Island, South Wales in 1966.

After the dreariness of wartime, Butlin provided a place where everything was colourful. His escapist vision for a nation still under austerity conditions was crowned by a motto from Shakespeare: 'Our true intent is all for your delight.' Visitors arrived at the camp's own railway halt where they and their luggage were transferred to a land train that delivered them, first to reception and then to their own chalet. This detached dwelling was not much bigger than a modern beach hut but it had central heating, the services of a chambermaid and, perhaps most crucially, it came with a key that allowed access at any point during the day. Many young couples, who had married during the uncertain conditions of wartime, closed the chalet door and experienced their first taste of domestic privacy. Children of the baby boomer generation were welcomed as guests in their own right. Unlike boarding houses, which were notoriously un-child-friendly, Butlin's provided bunk beds and playgrounds, kids' clubs and 'Aunties' and 'Uncles' whose sole purpose was to keep children entertained. The whole family could be occupied in different ways at the same time; it was a blissful release for post-war parents.

After the grey war years Billy Butlin provided a colourful holiday environment with brightly painted chalets set among rose gardens. His only Scottish holiday camp opened at Ayr in 1947. (Butlin's Archive)

Children under ten went half price and at Ayr under-fours were free. There were on-site crèche facilities and after children were put to bed the 'night-owl' chalet patrol did the rounds, listening for tears that were soothed by a nurse before any summons was made to mother on the camp's loud speaker system.

Responsibility for anything other than enjoyment was handed over at the Butlin gates. Even waking up was organised. At 7.30 each morning the chalet speakers crackled into life with the following cheery song:

Roll out of bed in the morning
With a big, big smile and a good, good morning.
You'll find life is worthwhile
If you roll out of bed with a smile.

A typical Butlin's dining room in the late 1940s. Food was still rationed so a team of girls was specially trained to cut the correct coupons from campers' ration books. Mealtimes were a highly organised exercise in mass catering. (Butlin's Archive)

Meals were served in immense dining halls but the highly efficient system of mass catering only worked if each sitting was ready at its appointed time. Divested of any need to consider when and what to eat, campers willingly accepted the regimentation this required. Recent experiences of military life meant they were used to being organised anyway. In the first season at Skegness, however, it became clear that creating a community required some artificial stimulus and so the Red Coat was born, a broker of social interaction in a crowd and a powerful corporate symbol that was transferred to Blue and Green Coats at Pontin's and Warner's respectively.

Participation was encouraged with numerous talent contests that saw people throw off their normal British reserve. As the top prize was often a free Butlin's holiday, people literally kept coming back for more. There was a category for everyone from Bonny Babies through Miss Lovely Legs to Knobbly Knees, Glamorous Grandmother and Shiniest Bald Head. Joining in also had its more energetic forms, whether proper sports or those like the egg 'n' spoon race that everyone knew from school days. There were swimming galas and donkey derbies. Vast theatres hosted plays, cabarets and to confound the critics a post-war season by the San Carlo Opera Company from Covent Garden. In the established tradition of seaside architecture, communal interiors were designed to stress glamour, fantasy and escape. Clacton's ballroom was described as 'one of the finest in England' with 'fairy tale castles as the walls and Tudor pillars supporting a centre balcony…' Only the beach drew campers beyond the perimeter fence; nearby resorts could not compete with the facilities at Butlin's in the halcyon days between 1946 and the early 1960s.

Although Butlin based his prices on the average weekly wage, a holiday at one of his camps during the first decade of operations was considered rather posh among ordinary working people. Chalets were filled by the ranks of lower and middle management rather than those from the factory floors, who were catered for by other chains or family-run camps. Fred Pontin came onto the holiday camp scene after a successful career on the Stock Exchange, via war work organising mass catering facilities. He realised that the coast, which had been out of bounds for several years, would take on a new attractiveness in peacetime. In 1946 he bought a pre-existing camp at Brean Sands near Burnham-on-Sea in Somerset and, after a quick revamp using war surplus from the Ministry of Works, he began welcoming visitors. Pontin received so many expressions of interest that he quickly also purchased the Brean Sands' sister camp at Osmington Bay near Weymouth.

Greetings from PONTIN'S
RIVIERA AT WEYMOUTH

The blonde girl in hot pants and heels helps give this Pontin's Holiday Centre a Mediterranean look at a time when more people were choosing to go abroad.

Within a year, he had acquired four more sites: Sand Bay at Weston-super-Mare, Buckleigh Place at Westward Ho!, the South Devon Holiday Camp near Paignton and Bracklesham Bay in Sussex. Pontin was now marketing 1,300 accommodation units over six locations compared to Butlin's five camps offering more than 30,000 bed spaces. The two entrepreneurs worked in friendly rivalry: Pontin's was always cheaper, its smaller sites benefiting from lower overheads, while Butlin's huge size gave campers more choice of entertainments. In the summer of 1965 a week's full board at Pontin's cost £10 per adult while the same package at Butlin's was £16.

By the early 1960s Britain had at least 100 holiday camps. Warner's went from eight at the beginning of the decade to eleven by 1965; Pontin's continued its acquisition and make-over policy, taking its empire up to sixteen; Butlin's stopped at nine but remained the market leader. The total attendance of all the other camps combined didn't even come close to the one million plus holidaymakers that headed to Butlin's every year. And yet it was Fred Pontin who set the agenda by reacting to the increasingly apparent desire for change and choice. He launched Pontinental Holidays to capitalise on interest in foreign destinations and embarked on new 'Rent-a-Chalet' camps at home. Guests had moved on from fixed meal times with traditional waitress service, so Pontin experimented with 'tray-and-away' systems that offered such novelties as salad bars and carousels stacked with different pudding choices. Chalets were also upgraded with en suite bathrooms and toilets while new more permanent brick-built accommodation featured fitted kitchens for self-catering. Butlin's was forced to follow after recording its first ever loss in 1965. The group offered bed and breakfast holidays from 1967 and began building self-contained, three-room flats. It also started converting the large chalets that had previously been let to parties of teenagers. All the big operators became less welcoming to groups of single boys or girls because of problems with gangs and vandalism, not to mention the rumours of orgies, which were putting off families.

By the 1970s wartime camaraderie was wearing thin and the Viennese ballrooms were looking shabby. Re-branding as holiday centres, villages or parks failed to address the huge change in people's expectations that Billy Butlin himself had helped to foster. The original snobbery against holiday camps re-emerged as they came to be seen as a low-class leisure option. All three of the big operators passed out of their original ownership, Butlin's in 1972, Pontin's in 1978 and Warner's in 1983. Yet despite downsizing the companies that helped change the face of British seaside accommodation continue to operate to this day.

RIGHT
Ready for a night out at Pontin's Osmington Bay in the swinging Sixties. These teenage girls lied about their age to get into an adults-only camp. (Vanessa Ferry)

BELOW
A 1960s guitar band prepares to play in the Pig and Whistle Bar at Barry Island. All entertainment was included within the Butlin's package. (John Hinde)

ABERYSTWYTH

THE BIARRITZ OF WALES

Chapter Six

SEA AND SUN BATHING

SEASIDE HOLIDAYS were special because they offered the thrill of doing things not possible at home; chief among these pastimes was sea bathing. Although it began as a health pursuit, bathing for pleasure really took off in the nineteenth century. At that time bathers were expected to pay for entry to the sea. It was socially unacceptable to get changed on the beach, so Victorian holidaymakers had to hire a bathing machine. Resembling a beach hut on wheels, these vehicles first appeared in the mid eighteenth century. They were designed to deliver people bathing on their doctor's orders directly into the sea. After paying the hire charge bathers would ascend a set of steps at the rear of the carriage, a horse would then be attached to the front and as the bathing machine was pulled forward the bather would attempt to undress ready to emerge down a second set of steps into the briny. Windows were either tiny or non-existent. Benches were provided along the side walls but because of the two doors at front and back they had to be quite narrow. There were pegs on which to hang dry clothes and hats, and sometimes a mirror, though its value must have been negligible in the machine's dark interior. Despite their discomforts the Victorians embraced bathing machines, in part as a way to maintain standards of decency on ever more crowded beaches.

Even before the railway age there had been a tacit separation of male and female bathers; from the mid nineteenth century keeping the sexes apart became a priority. Men retained the right to bathe naked, falling back on medical folklore that clothes hampered absorption of the sea's healthy mineral particles. The bathing machines used by women were consequently placed at a distance from those used by men to prevent any indecent anatomical exposure.

Resort authorities passed by-laws to determine the exact distance, but official demands for segregation met with mixed results. Margate Town Council finally gave in to pressure for regulation in 1862, decreeing that all bathers wear costumes and that a distance of not less than 60 feet be maintained between male and female machines. Two years later a local newspaper dismissed the rules as 'mere waste paper' and in 1866 protested that the sexes were still bathing together, that for every man wearing drawers there were ten who did not, and that defiance of the authorities continued because 'offenders know they will not prosecute.' Evidence from other places shows this situation was not unusual. A more effective form of division made use of coastal geography. At St Andrews in Fife the West Sands were for men only, the Castle Sands for women. In North Devon, the male and female bathing pools of Ilfracombe's Tunnels Beach were separated by a protruding cliff.

Family bathing was possible on quieter beaches where there was no likelihood of trippers dashing into the water in a naked free-for-all and therefore no need for

OPPOSITE
Aberystwyth's claim to be the 'Biarritz of Wales' is almost believable thanks to the streamlined figures on this 1930s guidebook.

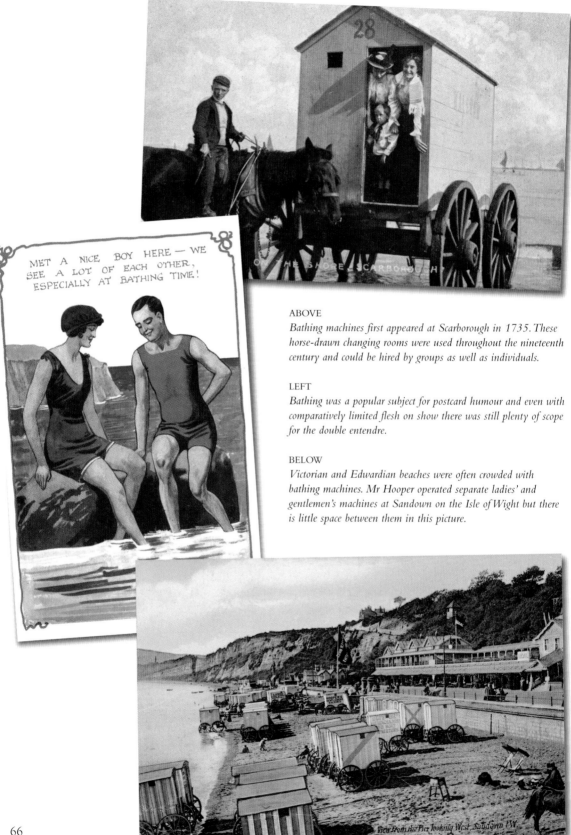

MET A NICE BOY HERE — WE SEE A LOT OF EACH OTHER, ESPECIALLY AT BATHING TIME!

ABOVE
Bathing machines first appeared at Scarborough in 1735. These horse-drawn changing rooms were used throughout the nineteenth century and could be hired by groups as well as individuals.

LEFT
Bathing was a popular subject for postcard humour and even with comparatively limited flesh on show there was still plenty of scope for the double entendre.

BELOW
Victorian and Edwardian beaches were often crowded with bathing machines. Mr Hooper operated separate ladies' and gentlemen's machines at Sandown on the Isle of Wight but there is little space between them in this picture.

MIXED BATHING

THREE CHEERS FOR THE RED, WHITE AND BLUE.

rules against it. The passing of by-laws was often motivated by social snobbery and a desire to control working-class visitors, even though the restrictions that divided mothers from sons and fathers from daughters applied to everyone. By the 1890s there was real disenchantment with the British way of doing things, particularly among those who had seen how their Continental cousins managed to bathe together without scandal. Mounting pressure led to a national press campaign in 1895–6 that saw petitions organised and local newspapers bombarded with letters demanding the relaxation of restrictive by-laws. The first resorts to act were those most likely to lose their wealthy clientele to more permissive foreign resorts. In 1895 Llandudno officially reintroduced mixed bathing on part of its beach, followed by Paignton in 1896. Paignton was not alone in finding that business boomed after it permitted men and women to bathe together in neck-to-knee costumes. Not all resorts were so easily convinced, but mixed bathing gradually became the norm as bathing machines were replaced by beach tents, then rows of permanent changing cubicles. 'Mackintosh bathing' also became more widespread, with people walking to the beach ready changed under their coats in order to avoid the cost of undressing in a council cabin. Resort authorities proved slow to give up on bathing as a revenue generator, but by 1939 the principle of charging for access to the sea had finally disappeared.

If attitudes about how to enter the water changed, so did expectations of what bathers should do when they got in. Sea bathing was definitely not the same thing as swimming. In the 1870s the majority of bathers could not swim and the total holiday time they spent in the water might be less than half an hour, the standard

Mixed bathing became acceptable from the 1890s as by-laws designed to keep men and women apart were gradually repealed. These patriotic gents certainly seem pleased with the change.

In a variation on 'mackintosh' bathing these girls in the 1920s wear towels gathered in like cloaks around their necks.

time for hire of a bathing machine. The eighteenth- and early-nineteenth-century pursuit of good health through bathing was really more about getting wet. Cold water dips designed to shock the system were prescribed by medics and administered by 'dippers', who were usually female and notoriously brawny. Even when bathing became associated with pleasure it was still largely restricted to splashing about outside the machine. Not till the 1860s and 70s did interest begin to grow in swimming as a means of propulsion and as a sport. The Brighton Swimming Club held its first races in 1861 open to male competitors, who were required to wear drawers. In Devon, the Dawlish Swimming Association was established in 1864 and its competitions soon became a highlight of the summer season. The exploits of Captain Matthew Webb, who became the first man ever to swim the Channel in 1875, also helped raise the profile of swimming and doubtless inspired many people to learn. At the seaside, lessons were often given by self-styled 'Professors of Natation' who drummed up custom by displaying their prowess as aquatic entertainers.

Professor Harry Parker was a local celebrity at Ilfracombe. He was 'Champion Swimmer of England' for three years from 1870 and initiated his son Harry Junior into the art of fancy swimming at a young age so that the two could perform together. Harry Junior's repertoire comprised such tricks as diving and coming up feet first, eating, drinking and writing under water, and imitations of marine life including crab, porpoise and octopus. His handcuff escape was dubbed 'The most daring feat ever attempted in the sea'. Other artistes specialised in stunt dives. The West Pier at Brighton could boast several such performers including Professor Reddish who was famed for diving off on a bicycle and Zoe Brigden, renowned

Aquatic entertainers were popular all around the coast. Professor Harry Parker and his son amazed spectators for many years at Ilfracombe in North Devon. (Tunnel's Beach Ilfracombe)

for her 'wooden soldier' dive in which she plunged head first into the sea with arms at her sides. During the Edwardian era, Professor Osbourne launched himself off the roof of Thom's Tea House on Southport Pier and at New Brighton inter-war steamers were welcomed by Peggy, a man with a peg leg, whose daring dive off the wooden pier was made just moments before the boat docked. The Lady Diver of Herne Bay performed during the 1930s, while Professor Twigg and his son did the rounds of Yorkshire resorts in the pre- and post-war period. In the off-season they worked as miners in the West Riding, returning to the coast each summer for popular performances including Professor Twigg the Younger smoking underwater off Whitby pier.

Professor Osbourne prepares to leap from the roof of Thom's Tea House on Southport Pier. The back of this 1903 postcard reads, 'I saw the dive today at 12 o'clock, it was very good.'

Most holidaymakers were considerably less ambitious and the simple joys of paddling were well known to young and old alike. Going for a paddle was like a free taster of the cooling sea and for day trippers, who could afford neither the expense nor the time of queuing for a bathing machine, it was the next best thing to a proper dip. Though some stripped off in contravention of the rules, the majority made do with rolling up their trouser legs and hitching up their skirts. Paddling has remained a popular seaside treat, good for a giggle without the need to undress.

At the more adventurous end of the spectrum there was surfing. The first time a Briton touched a surfboard was in Hawaii around 1778, when at least one of Captain James Cook's crew tried a native's wooden craft. Scattered references to

Paddlers have been rolling up their trousers and hitching up their skirts for generations, so these 1950s holidaymakers are following a well-established tradition.

Children in rubber rings splash in the waves at Bognor Regis in 1974.

surfing on British shores crop up over the ensuing century, most notably from English swimming champion Charles Steedman who wrote about using a 5-foot surfboard in 1867. The number of enthusiasts grew significantly after the First World War and in the 1930s surf riding began to develop as a serious sport. Pioneers made their own longboards and tried Hawaiian stand-up surfing, while holidaymakers were happy to ride the waves on their bellies, hiring short wooden planks at Cornish resorts like Newquay and Bude. Thanks to the advent of lighter materials like balsa, fibreglass and foam, surfing as we know it took off in the late 1950s and early 1960s, drawing a small but dedicated band of followers for an alternative seaside experience.

The move towards a more active bathing experience created demand for a suitable type of costume. Women experienced the greatest advances, progressing from the full-body suit of bloomers and jacket to the bikini. In the 1860s, ankle-length bloomers represented an improvement on the old type of bathing gown, which was little more than a shapeless sack gathered at the neck and sleeves. Unfortunately the heavy serge and flannel used to make mid-nineteenth-century suits hampered movement, so by the late 1870s trousers had become knee-length and considerations of fashion had begun to influence styles and colours. As women's bathing suits got progressively smaller men's got bigger, going from nothing to short briefs then full-body costumes, until both sexes were wearing a similar one-piece garment that came down to the elbows and knees. Mixed bathing made costumes more visible but as early twentieth-century photographs show, attempts to create a flattering shape were hindered by the available materials. The reality for most people was a hired costume stitched with the name of the bathing machine proprietor or the local council.

During the Victorian period bare flesh was unfashionable and genteel ladies protected their pale countenances with parasols because tanned skin carried

The reality of sun bathing on the beach at Great Yarmouth in 1938.

This little girl wears a swimming costume knitted by her mother in the 1950s. Homemade garments were fine until they got wet and the wool stretched! (Vanessa Ferry)

overtones of manual labour. As wealthy women took part in more open-air sports like tennis and cycling, this prevailing attitude began to change. Around the turn of the century European experiments in the use of sun treatment for tuberculosis also led to a growing belief in the health benefits of ultra violet rays. According to the historical evidence, Coco Chanel did not 'invent' sun bathing, but when she walked down the gangway of the Duke of Westminster's yacht 'brown as a cabin boy' in 1923 she immediately made a minority pastime chic. Following her lead the Bright Young Things of inter-war Europe lay bronzing their bodies for hours on the beaches of the French Riviera and, despite the uncertain British climate, sun bathing rapidly caught on. Inter-war guidebooks carried adverts for sun tan lotions, hotels built new sun terraces and special glass was fitted in the windows of Cornish Riviera Express trains so that passengers could soak up ultra violet rays as they sped to the Southwest. Resorts competed for the best sunshine statistics to win custom among holidaymakers keen to spend lazy days on the beach. In 1929 Aberystwyth claimed to be the 'sunniest spot in the British Isles' with 1,862.0 annual sunshine hours compared to just 1,677.3 in Blackpool. And as foreign destinations became gradually more accessible in the post-war years, resorts gave even higher billing to the sun in their adverts and catchphrases. In 1956 visitors were invited to 'Stay with the sun at

Eastbourne', the 'Sun trap of the south', while there was 'something for everyone at sunny Worthing', top of the list being sunshine. This huge cultural shift changed the way people used the beach as well as the amount of clothing considered decent.

Women's greater freedom of dress after the First World War helped to ensure that by the end of the 1920s bathing costumes had taken on a more recognisably modern form. The one-piece suit was now made of figure-hugging machine-knitted wool, often cut low at the back and with the sides scooped out to help maximise tan-ability. In 1929 manufacturers Jantzen went so far as to claim their newest women's model as the 'the suit that changed bathing into swimming'. With shoulder straps instead of sleeves, shorts cut just below the top of the leg and no overskirt it created a streamlined silhouette. After the Second World War the seaside was even busier, so the market for bathing costumes increased and prices began to fall. This was the era of the notorious knitted swimsuit, remembered for its sagginess by many among the baby-boomer generation. Magazines like *Stitchcraft* offered patterns for the whole post-war family, including belted trunks for father. It was a far cry from the Hollywood glamour of 1950s swimwear, with buxom beach babes pictured in the latest styles. Modern stretch fabrics have given swimming costumes the comfort, ease of movement and flattering lines that former generations couldn't quite achieve but the last great innovation was the bikini, first launched to a shocked world in 1946 and adopted by the mainstream in the 1960s. Young women took advantage of a more permissive society to reduce their seaside costume to three small triangles and haven't looked back since.

At the same time as sun bathing took off, a new type of structure appeared at seaside resorts around the country. Lidos epitomised the spirit of the 1930s: healthy exercise in the fresh air, sun worship, the mass cult of leisure in which everyone could be a consumer, all wrapped up in the clean forms of Modern architecture. With a limitless supply of bathing water on hand it might seem strange that seaside

A selection of 1940s swimsuits modelled by friends at Margate. Neither the male nor female costumes are terribly flattering.

resorts embraced this new leisure facility so ardently, but that they created some of the largest and most costly says a lot about the intense competition to lure holidaymakers. The South Bay Bathing Pool at Scarborough was one of the earliest, opening in July 1915. The idea was to provide a safe bathing place even when the sea was rough and to earn revenue from swimming galas and festivals. In the inter-war period, resorts as far apart as Troon in Scotland and Penzance in Cornwall built on this precedent. By 1933 Scarborough's pool looked out-of-date enough to require modernisation works, foremost among them being the construction of a concrete diving stage, a must-have item for any lido. The apogee was reached at Weston-super-Mare in 1937 with seven elegant boards cantilevered from two reinforced concrete arches. Described as the 'finest diving platform in Europe' it immediately became synonymous with the town.

Each new lido made its own unique claims. The Blackpool Open Air Baths opened in 1923 with tiered seating for 3,000 spectators and dressing rooms for 574 bathers, built along a concourse that measured a third of a mile. Southport got its Sea Bathing Lake in 1928, a 'magnificent temple … built to the goddess of air and water and sunshine.' In 1933 the south coast resort of Hastings dared to challenge the northern giants with a D-shaped bathing pool at St Leonards-on-Sea that could accommodate 2,500 spectators and had a gymnasium, rooftop sun terrace and underground car park. Two years later Tinside Lido was created under the rocky cliffs of Plymouth Hoe and in 1936 Edinburgh's seaside resort, Portobello, claimed the first outdoor pool in Britain to have a wave machine. The peak of the lido craze came, however, when Morecambe

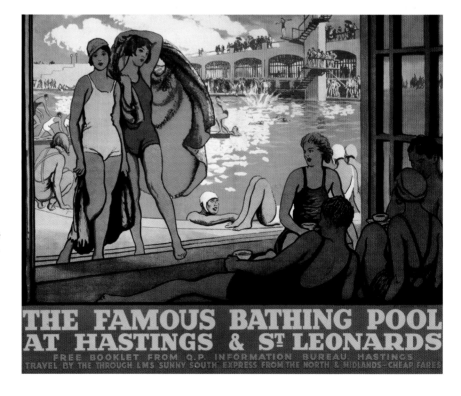

The lido was the must-have resort accessory of the inter-war years. The open-air Bathing Pool at St Leonards in Sussex opened in 1933 having cost the huge sum of £60,000. (National Railway Museum / Science & Society Picture Library)

THE FAMOUS BATHING POOL AT HASTINGS & St LEONARDS
FREE BOOKLET FROM Q.P. INFORMATION BUREAU, HASTINGS
TRAVEL BY THE THROUGH LMS SUNNY SOUTH EXPRESS FROM THE NORTH & MIDLANDS - CHEAP FARES

attempted to move out from under the shadow of its near neighbour Blackpool, by unveiling its £130,000 Super Swimming Stadium in July 1936. To repay this huge investment the lido had to be about more than swimming, so cafés were provided for the thousands of spectators who came to watch on ordinary days as well as for galas, diving displays and water polo matches. Bands played regularly and the combined effect of music and water was most charming at night when the pools were illuminated.

Another lido staple was the beauty contest. Margate's sea water pool opened at Cliftonville in 1927 and three years later played host to weekly parades of female holidaymakers. Girls entered for a lark and as many of them came dressed in hired costumes a big incentive to taking part must have been the chance of winning the top prize of a bathing costume of their own. Different aspects of feminine charm were judged each week and contests included Miss Calf and Ankle, Miss Mermaid, Miss Lovely Legs and Miss Grace and Bearing, for which contestants were required to parade around the pool carrying a Grecian urn. At the opening of the Weston-super-Mare pool in 1937 spectators were treated to 'Mannequin Parades' showing the latest swimsuit styles including the 'Ribbolastic' and 'Windsor Water Woollies'. After the war, visitors were invited to compete for the title of 'Modern Venus', a free-to-enter beauty contest that took place at Weston pool every Thursday in July. The biggest event, however, began at Morecambe's Super Swimming Stadium in the summer of 1945, just weeks after VE day. Over 4,000 people attended the grand final, which was later renamed 'Miss Great Britain'. Throughout the 1950s and 60s many young women enjoyed a brief moment of glory with a winner's sash draped over their bathing costume.

The winner and contestants of a Miss Lido competition at Cliftonville in the 1960s. Carrying the Grecian urns was supposed to enhance the contestants' 'grace and bearing'. (John Hinde)

Chapter Seven

ON THE BEACH

T HE BEACH was not just about bathing. By the mid nineteenth century it had become a leisure location in its own right. Seaside holidaymakers placed an increasing premium on beach time, whether it was actively spent in walking, riding, playing games and digging, or more contemplative pursuits like reading, chatting and watching. To sit or lie in the salty breeze was as wonderfully unfamiliar as the feeling of sand underfoot, turning simple pleasures into something out of the ordinary. So many things that we associate with the British seaside belong to the beach; donkeys and deckchairs, rock pools and sand castles, Punch and Judy, and buckets and spades.

All of the above have been handed down from our Victorian forbears, yet monochrome photographs give a false impression of their beach experience. Long exposure times emptied the black and white sands of their vibrancy, condemning our ancestors to appear static, if not downright dour. In fact, the reverse was true. The Victorian beach was colourful, noisy, busy and brash. Thousands of people spewing from excursion trains represented a huge captive audience for the salesmen and entertainers who turned the sands into an improvised playground-cum-market place. All manner of refreshments could be bought from specialist vendors who criss-crossed the beach loudly touting their wares. Some of the shouts heard at Great Yarmouth in 1877 included: 'Here's your chocolate creams. Buns two a penny. Yarmouth rock a penny a bar. Apples penny a bag… Lemonade threepence a bottle. Pears or grapes, all ripe, buy a nice bunch of grapes, Sir. Walnuts eight a penny, fine walnuts. Milk, penny a glass.' Blackpool beach was even more crowded, as an 1895 survey by the Town Clerk revealed. Among the 316 'standings on the foreshore' there were sixty-two fruit vendors, fifty-seven stalls selling toys, general goods and jewellery, fifty-two ice cream stalls, forty-seven vendors of sweets and refreshments and twenty-one oyster and prawn dealers.

Ice cream was an enduring favourite, transformed from an expensive and rare treat to a seaside staple thanks to late-nineteenth century developments in industrial refrigeration. Many of the makers were Italian following the precedent of Carlo Gatti, a Swiss-Italian businessman who opened Britain's first ice cream stall outside London's Charing Cross station in 1851. His successors followed the crowds to the beach where they dealt in the 'penny lick', a fixed price scoop served in a glass. Designed with a shallow depression on top of a thick glass base this container appeared to hold more than it actually did, disappointing many an expectant customer. Concerns about the hygiene of re-usable glasses saw the ice cream cone emerge as an edible replacement in the Edwardian era. It has yet to be bettered and from the mid-1920s was being sold by the Wall's 'Stop and buy one' man who dispensed his cool flavours from a tricycle, the forerunner of modern ice cream vans. The much-loved and peculiarly British '99' ice cream was born soon after, taking its name from the specially shortened stick of chocolate produced for the ice cream trade by Cadbury and launched as the 'Flake 99' in 1930. Twenty years later a chemical research team, whose members included a young Margaret Thatcher, developed a way to double the amount of air in ice cream, reducing the cost of ingredients and paving the way for Mr Whippy, a perfect partner for the chocolate flake.

In addition to refreshment vendors the Victorian beach boasted a plethora of showmen. In 1895 Blackpool played host to thirty-six photographers and exhibitors of 'photographs, kinetoscopes, picture views, stereoscopes and telescopes,' twenty-four ventriloquists and phrenologists, six quack doctors, six musicians and five conjurors. Thanks to developments in photographic technology, late nineteenth-century visitors were able to return home with a visual record of their time by the sea, perhaps one that showed their heads peeking through a painted board as if on another person's body! As their equipment became more portable, photographers were able to roam the beach taking snapshots, which were then quickly and cheaply made ready for purchase, often in postcard format. Not until cameras became truly affordable in the 1950s did this beach trade cease. The quack doctors with their miraculous potions, the chiropodists who cut excursionists' corns in front of an admiring audience, and the phrenologists with their ability to read character by examining head bumps proved to be more short-lived.

Beach stalls were increasingly subject to licensing and at Weston-super-Mare protests against the 'veritable pandemonium' on the sands led to their number being restricted to fifty in 1912. Some booths relocated to the promenade or the pier, though many remained on the fringes of what resort authorities considered acceptable. In 1925 Madame Winter was fined for telling fortunes at Gorleston. It was no coincidence that Madame Sato, a palmist who had been working at neighbouring Great Yarmouth, packed up her stand on Britannia Pier and disappeared at the same time. By contrast, the Punch and Judy man proved to be one of the few beach entertainers who were always welcome. With his cast of glove puppets, and trademark striped theatre, he moved to the coast from inland fairgrounds, performing a show that had its origins in sixteenth-century Italy and the *commedia dell'arte* tradition. Diarist Samuel Pepys recorded seeing Punchinello as a marionette in the 1660s but it was only after his strings were cut that he became the portable Mr Punch, joined from the 1800s by a stock cast of well-known characters from his long-suffering wife Judy to the Crocodile and Policeman. Every puppeteer, known as the Professor, brought his own style to the performance, the skill of the spectacle often passed from father to son. The Codman family's Punch and Judy show first appeared on the promenade at Llandudno in the 1860s, their version of Mr Punch's 'That's the way to do it!' still going into the fourth generation and the twenty-first century.

Seaside donkeys also boast a pre-Victorian heritage, being ridden at Margate from the 1790s and rapidly becoming popular among the fashionable ladies of Brighton. They provided a more sedate alternative to Georgian horse-racing, still possible on beaches that were otherwise only frequented by walkers and bathing machines. As resorts grew so did the number of donkeys, some pulling carriages across the sands or

ABOVE: *A tintype photograph of three generations on the Victorian beach. All are dressed in heavy layers and hats – even the little girls in their archetypal sailor suits.*

RIGHT: *Relaxing in front of a refreshment kiosk on Margate beach. The advertisements are not for food or drink but for brands of popular 1930s cigarettes.*

BELOW: *The Victorian beach as market place. Itinerant food vendors, photographers, phrenologists and fairground operators were among the stallholders on the sands at places like Swansea.*

Edwardian donkey boys were a familiar sight in their uniform of bare feet, rolled-up trousers, waistcoat, neckerchief and flat cap. Donkeys have been giving rides across the beach since the late eighteenth century.

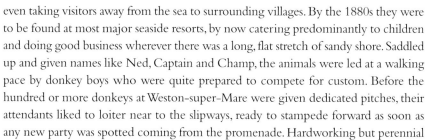

Buckets, boats and fishing nets have helped make the rock pool a children's playground for over a century. The Edwardian infants in this illustration came from a wealthy family but seaside toys became more affordable after the First World War.

even taking visitors away from the sea to surrounding villages. By the 1880s they were to be found at most major seaside resorts, by now catering predominantly to children and doing good business wherever there was a long, flat stretch of sandy shore. Saddled up and given names like Ned, Captain and Champ, the animals were led at a walking pace by donkey boys who were quite prepared to compete for custom. Before the hundred or more donkeys at Weston-super-Mare were given dedicated pitches, their attendants liked to loiter near to the slipways, ready to stampede forward as soon as any new party was spotted coming from the promenade. Hardworking but perennial favourites, seaside donkeys had witnessed significant improvements in their working conditions by the 1980s when rides were made contingent on weight, working hours were regulated and days off became obligatory, an overdue acknowledgement of the pleasure given by these animals to millions of British children.

Other, much smaller, creatures also captivated children's attention, scooped out of rock pools into waiting buckets. For a time the study of seaweed, shells and rocks was a veritable craze among middle-class holidaymakers, led by publications that revealed nature's coastal wonderland and instructed readers on how to recreate it at home in aquaria. Based on his investigations along the Devon coast, the naturalist Philip Henry Gosse wrote a series of beautifully illustrated shore books during the 1850s, inspiring a passion for amateur marine biology that had the unfortunate side-effect of denuding some coastal stretches of all rock pool life. Interest had peaked by the 1870s, satisfied thereafter by large public aquariums and the shell grottoes that became a feature of numerous resorts. At that point the fishing and shrimping nets were handed over to children.

The Sands, Weymouth

An impressive example of sandcastle building from Edwardian Weymouth. This double-decker fortress was created by a sand artist but amateurs could test their skill in sandcastle-building competitions.

The simple pleasures of moulding and building in sand had always been the domain of young beach-goers. In the mid- to late-nineteenth century, tin buckets and wooden spades tended to be the property of more prosperous children. When the market for seaside toys expanded after the First World War they became available to all. Cutting into firm sand, patting it into a nearly full bucket, upending it and then slowly revealing the castle beneath has always proved a satisfying pastime. Then there was the moat to make, destined to remain empty however many trips were made to fetch water, a bit of tunnelling and some battlements, all topped off with a paper flag.

"Look what I've found, Mummie!"

During the Second World War beaches were covered in barbed wire to resist possible invasion. Even after fighting ended, unexploded mines were a genuine hazard, so it is hardly surprising that this little boy's curiosity has made his mother feel faint.

Most sandcastles were made for fun but competitions also proved popular. Areas of sand were marked off, a time limit was set and all the young entrants got a prize. In July 1903 eighty boys and girls took part in the Bovril-sponsored sand design competition at Great Yarmouth. Some beaches had more regular displays sculpted by professional sand artists, with 30-foot-long tableaux, ranging from 'The Last Supper' to the 'Mad Hatter's Tea Party', still being created at Weymouth into the 1970s. Post-war families relaxing on the beach turned sand into modern shapes including boats, cars and planes as well as the traditional castle. They also passed on the well-established beach habit of burying relations in the sand, a firm favourite up to the present day.

As the incoming tide washed away the day's building activity, messages written in the sand were also erased. Some were childish scribbles but others were heartfelt declarations of love. The holiday romance was nothing new when Charles Dickens wrote about it in his novel *Bleak House*: 'It is the hottest long vacation known for many years. All the young clerks are madly in love, and, according to their various degrees, pine for bliss with the beloved object at Margate, Ramsgate or Gravesend.' Buttoned-up Brits have been taking advantage of the informal seaside atmosphere for generations, helping to make saucy postcards a best-selling institution in the process. A brief stay heightened the erotic urgency and normal rules didn't apply. If it was impossible to smuggle a new girlfriend back to the boarding house then there was always the beach to serve as night-time rendezvous for amorous couples.

As well as castles, sand could also be sculpted into more modern shapes like this sand boat made by Michael and Brian Ferry at Lowestoft in the mid-1950s.
(Doreen Ferry)

The seaside has long been a backdrop for holiday romance with the moonlit beach, parodied in this 1940s postcard, a popular choice among lovers.

By the late 1940s Blackpool had gained a reputation as the country's seaside sex capital; the sand under the North Pier was notorious. Whatever went on under cover of darkness, the beach by day was a great place for flirtations. Bathing offered a unique opportunity to see bodies that were normally hidden; early-twentieth-century costumes were ostensibly designed for maximum cover, but they left little to the imagination when wet. Other beach sports also provided the chance to show off, making games of cricket, leapfrog and tug-of-war particularly popular among groups of single holidaymakers.

This type of activity relied on comfortable clothes and the gradual change to more casual attire is a key indicator of how social changes were reflected on the beach between 1870 and 1970. Until the inter-war period most ordinary people had work clothes and 'Sunday Best'; leisurewear was unnecessary when there was so little leisure. Since a trip to the seaside was a treat, it was seen as an occasion to dress up. Men wore a suit and tie, women the most fashionable dress they could afford, one that covered the neck, wrist and ankle. Everyone wore hats. From the 1890s straw boaters became the up-to-date male choice. They were superseded by panama hats and by the 1920s no hats at all. Working men, however, stuck to their flat caps. Ideas of what was considered smart differed between the classes and it was a paradox that holidaymakers with money generally wore less than those without. Youth really began to dictate the style agenda after the First World War with white flannel trousers, stripy blazers and

Working men remained smartly dressed on the beach and flat caps were part of the expected outfit during the 1920s, though this wouldn't stop them helping with the sandcastle building. (Gail Durbin)

Corporation attendants issued tickets for deckchair hire like this one from Eastbourne. It has been punched for an evening hire period valid between six and ten o'clock.

open-necked shirts being joined in the 1930s by Oxford bags, plus fours and short sleeves. Older men continued to wear braces, waistcoats, collars and ties, the taboo on body exposure lasting until well into the 1950s, when the jacket might come off when it was really hot but never the shirt and tie. Bare chests finally began their rise to popularity in the more permissive Sixties.

Women went from easy-fitting skirt and blouse combinations in the Edwardian era to the liberation of 1920s beach pyjamas, first worn on the French Riviera. In vivid coloured cottons or *crêpe de Chine*, these trouser and jacket sets were made for wearing over bathing costumes and were often teamed with floppy straw hats and high heels. It was not always easy to recreate the sophistication of Juan les Pins at British resorts like Clacton and Morecambe and as factory girls on works outings tried, beach pyjamas began to lose their glamour. Most women wore everyday cotton dresses with hems that gradually got shorter, their hats replaced by head scarves, if at all. Full skirts and shorts came in after the war, followed by miniskirts and hot pants.

Though beach fashions changed markedly the desire for relaxation remained the same. The very shape of the deckchair was calculated to induce laziness and its introduction at Margate in 1898 gave the seaside its own distinctive furniture. Until that point visitors had had to make do with the sand or old chairs from the kitchens

Deckchairs became standard beach furniture after their introduction at Margate in 1898. Though they had a reputation for being tricky to assemble, their canvas seats were perfect for reclining on the beach.

and bedrooms of locals. Set out in rows for hire, these rickety specimens only allowed for an upright position that now seems unnaturally rigid for a seaside setting. The deckchair got its name from widespread use on passenger ships but had its origins with the British Army in India, where it was developed as a type of collapsible camp furniture. Cheap to produce, easy to store and move, it quickly proved itself on the beach and by the late 1940s Margate was making 2.1 million deckchair hires every season. Only Edwardian Rhyl seems to have experimented with different beach seating, introducing wicker chairs that, thanks to a hood that came up over the seat, resembled nothing so much as large peanuts. They were common on Dutch beaches but came to nothing in North Wales.

Once the beach-goer had grappled with assembly of the deckchair there was little to do but lie back and watch the world go by. There was always activity to catch the eye, whether from frolicking bathers, playing children or working fishermen. As the crowds grew, these latter individuals and their apparatus of boats and nets were pushed away from the resort centre. At Hastings they were tidied off the main beach onto the Stade, where the tall black net huts made the backdrop to a more picturesque setting for the visitors' curiosity. Where the lack of a harbour meant landing the catch on the beach or not at all, boat owners could supplement their income by offering pleasure rides and fishing trips during the season. At a village like Beer in Devon, twentieth-century holidaymakers were actually attracted by a wish to see the working boats that were disappearing elsewhere. As a break from people-watching, there was always reading – maybe the newspaper or the latest sensational novel. This too was a habit enjoyed by the Victorians, although the following quotation from *The Cornhill Magazine* of 1861

Clarice sat writing this postcard to Mabel as the tide came in on Southend beach. She wryly observed that 'this is no place for a quiet holiday, as you can see.' The pleasure yachts are as packed as the sands.

SOUTHEND-ON-SEA. Beach and Pleasure Yachts.

By the 1970s there was more flesh on show at the beach. The crowds at Bognor Regis included topless sunbathers and people on sun loungers instead of deckchairs.

suggests that good intentions have always been foiled by the relaxed atmosphere of the beach:

> Reading is supposed to be a favourite pastime at the sea-side, but this is a mistake; for although there is always a circulating library, and large quantities of novels, magazines, and books of travel are carried down to the beach each day by the ladies, they don't read them. They may open a volume, perhaps, and then they go to sleep for certain.

On sunny summer days the beach was packed and latecomers would struggle to find a bit of spare sand. By the second half of the twentieth century, beach towels and stripy windbreaks had been adopted as territory markers but the really lucky people were those who had the use of a beach hut. Bathing machines were phased out from the 1890s, so their role as changing accommodation was taken over first by tents and then by huts. The advantage in both cases was that these structures could be hired for longer periods of time – a day, a week or the whole season – therefore providing a little home from home. Accounts of Edwardian beach huts at upmarket resorts like Bexhill and Felixstowe focus on how the ritual of afternoon tea was transferred to the sands thanks to these convenient shelters. As bed and breakfast became a favoured accommodation option, the beach hut came into its own. It didn't matter if the boarding house door was locked when you had somewhere to take cover from the rain and brew up a nice cuppa. Long rows of brightly coloured huts were built around the coast during the 1920s and 30s, though some dating from this era were originally conceived by local

The James family from Winchmore Hill, north London, on the beach at Westcliffe-on-Sea, Essex in 1960. (Mr and Mrs Stanley James)

councils as short-hire changing cubicles, only being turned into day chalets after the Second World War. Built of brick or concrete, these bathing stations usually featured an integral café to replace the beach stalls that were on their way out. These cafés frequently advertised 'Trays for the beach', so if you didn't have the luxury of a hut you could still enjoy a cup of tea in your deckchair.

Felixstowe had Britain's earliest beach huts in the 1890s. Here they are seen in 1933 behind holidaymakers dressed in the latest casual styles.

CATLIN'S FAVOURITE PIERROTS

PIERROTS ON THE SANDS

Chapter Eight

OUTSIDE ENTERTAINMENTS

B RITISH SEASIDE resorts were constantly trying to outdo each other with attractions that would entice holidaymakers back each year. The fact that towns with pebble beaches could prosper proves that there was much more to the seaside than a strip of sand. From the later Victorian period attention focused upon the promenade and its transformation into a thoroughfare that was different from any to be found inland. Municipal spending increased as new walkways were created, gardens were planted and outdoor music venues were formalised. There were games to play, sights to see, and when night fell, the power of electricity was harnessed to turn the seafront into a twinkling version of its daytime self.

All around the coast there are esplanades, promenades and marine parades, their basic function as defensive sea wall turned into a virtue through the creation of that special place, the 'seafront'. In the early twentieth century, Blackpool laid three miles of broad new esplanades at a cost of £390,000. Bournemouth Corporation completed its Undercliff Drive in 1908, providing a 30-foot-wide carriage drive and 20-foot-wide promenade complete with the country's first municipal beach huts. Architectural furnishings in the shape of ornamental iron railings, lamp-brackets cast in the shape of sea creatures, open-sided shelters, public seats, kiosks and bandstands added to the sense of the seaside promenade as a distinct location. In the 1930s concrete replaced cast iron as the favoured material and Hastings got its impressive Double-Deck Parade extending westwards along the shore. The upper section was at road level while underneath was a covered walkway with seats provided in glass-fronted bays. Embellishments were not only structural. In the mid-1950s, weekend visitors to Brighton enjoyed the presence of glamorous Promettes who patrolled the promenade dressed in mist blue uniforms with cerise piping. It is a sign of a different era that as well as dispensing tourist information they also carried cigarette lighters in their specially designed handbags.

But what was the Promenade for? It was a place to take the air, see and be seen, saunter with family and friends, join in the jostle and bustle of the seaside crowds. There were also times when promenading turned into a social ritual and at some Victorian and Edwardian resorts the 'Church Parade' was an institution. After Sunday morning service, Scarborough's most elevated visitors gathered on the esplanade overlooking the South Bay and Spa, the women dressed as if for a fashion show. At Brighton, Sunday promenaders took to the 'world-famed Lawns' along the seafront, while at Ilfracombe they strolled below the rocky Capstone Hill. Resort authorities took note of the fact that holidaymakers spent a lot of their time wandering and landscaped other spaces to cater for this habit. Torquay had its Rock Walk, Bournemouth its Pine Walk and in 1893 Ramsgate got Madeira Walk, a path

OPPOSITE
In their distinctive white costumes with trademark black pompoms, Pierrots were a common seaside sight from 1900 to 1914. Will Catlin, manager of this troupe at Scarborough, produced Pierrot shows throughout northern England and Wales.

The 'Church Parade' had become a seaside institution by the early twentieth century. At Ilfracombe visitors walked around Capstone Hill after Sunday service.

from the cliff top to the beach where the naked chalk was adorned with artificial rock features, carefully chosen plants and even a waterfall powered by gas-engine. The zig-zag path was another cliff enhancement that sought to be practical and picturesque: by cutting a gentle meander into the cliff face at places like Bournemouth, Folkestone and Cromer it made the steep ascent more manageable.

Open spaces were a core attraction and during the first half of the twentieth century a great deal of municipal investment went into parks and gardens. At the 1913 opening of its newly landscaped seafront, Clacton council was congratulated for 'replacing the winkle and eel-pie shops previously down either side of the pier

All seaside resorts spent money on parks and gardens, often with an exotic theme. Alongside its urns and statuary, Poole's Italian Garden also had carpet planting, made popular by the Victorians. (John Hinde)

The cover of Torquay's
1966 guidebook suggests
it has something for
everyone with plenty of
outdoor activities and
enough hours of sunshine
to wear a bikini.

gap with beautiful flower beds and the bridge which stretched from cliff to cliff.'
Carpet gardens were a favourite and Eastbourne's famously manicured beds date
from the mid-1890s when the private floral displays of a seafront hotel were taken
into Corporation ownership. The Victorians were keen gardeners and their love for
bright, vibrant colour led to a passion for textile-inspired planting. Vast numbers of
exotic species were imported from all over the world and many eventually made
their way into seaside horticulture, frequently as part of ornamental displays or even
spelling out messages of welcome. The most obvious symbol of exoticism was the
palm tree, those planted at Torquay from the 1920s helping to reinforce the town's
claim to be the centre of the English Riviera. Foreign references helped add to the
holidaymakers' sense of being far away from home, so Poole was just one among
many places to boast an Italian garden, full of classical-looking statuary, urns and
temples. At Peasholm Park beside Scarborough's North Bay, the council planted

Music was a constant accompaniment to seaside life and brass bands were especially popular. Holidaymakers relaxed in deckchairs around bandstands like this elaborate birdcage example at Southend.

Japanese gardens. A bridge designed 'in the Japanese manner' led across the park's large ornamental lake to an island with a pagoda. In fact all the park buildings followed this theme, even the floating bandstand.

Wherever you went at the seaside there was some sort of musical accompaniment. The hurdy-gurdy men with their monkeys, accordionists, one-man bands and players on spoons all busked for the holidaymakers' pennies. It is no coincidence that the popular tune 'Oh I do like to be beside the seaside' gives prides of place to a stroll along the prom, 'Where the brass band plays, tiddly-om-pom-pom!' In 1889 the country had some 40,000 brass bands providing a quintessential working-class entertainment in the days before radio and television. Bandstands and band enclosures became a common sight along the seafront, often with oriental details like at Brighton or decorated with elaborate cast iron like the birdcage bandstand

A crowd gathers to watch minstrels perform on a temporary stage near the pier at Colwyn Bay. The original black American minstrels took London by storm in 1843.

at Southend. Sitting inside, the uniformed and moustachioed musicians often belonged to German bands, a ubiquitous feature of British seaside resorts until their rapid disappearance in 1914.

Alongside the German bands there were other groups of musical entertainers who relied on an imported formula for their seaside success. In 1843 a troupe of genuine black American minstrels took London by storm. Their plantation songs were immediately popular and widely copied, especially at the seaside where blacked-up imitators remained a continuous presence for the next fifty years. Wearing baggy trousers and bow ties these all-male companies played cornets, concertinas, 'bones' and a new instrument called the banjo. A character known as 'Uncle' drummed up business, encouraging children to participate and leading the audience as they joined in with songs like 'Swanee River', 'Golden Slipper' or other home-grown ballads. Comic relief was provided by the straight man Mr Interlocutor, and as the crowds gathered round the temporary stage one of the minstrels would act as 'bottler', with the important job of soliciting pennies.

Around 1900, minstrels were ousted by French-inspired Pierrots dressed in loose silk blouses and pantaloons and wearing conical hats, the whole ensemble topped off with trademark black pom poms. The Pierrot show was a mixture of short comical and musical acts, usually presented by six or seven men – though there was the occasional Pierrette – accompanied by a pianist. During the season they gave three or four performances a day on a temporary wooden stage. At resorts like Skegness, Silloth and Llandudno audiences gathered around the Pierrots in an open-air amphitheatre known as Happy Valley. Troupe names reflected their reputation for light-hearted fun: Saltburn had the 'Jovial Jollies', Rhyl the 'Quaintesques' and Ramsgate the 'Bohemians'. So successful did this form of seaside entertainment prove that a number of managers made their fortune by running Pierrot empires. The best-known was Will Catlin, who started out in Scarborough in 1895 and went on to conquer the rest of the east coast before taking on the Northwest. The novelty had worn off by the First World War and though the open-air theatrics continued,

In 1909 Gold's Smart Serenaders played three times a day on Margate sands. This promotional card also lists special events including children's talent competitions with 'Handsome prizes'.

There was a tennis craze in the 1920s and 30s which saw courts appear on seafronts around the country, as in this view of Felixstowe in Suffolk. Other sports like bowls and croquet were also catered for.

the performers were re-branded as concert parties. Jack Sheppard's Pierrots became Jack Sheppard's Brighton Entertainers with the men now in blazers, white trousers and yachting caps and the women in smart dresses and cloche hats.

As with entertainments, there was also a range of sports on offer at the seaside. Tennis became a seaside craze in the 1880s and young men were rarely to be seen without their racquets. Bernard Becker, the author of *Holiday Haunts*, found Eastbourne swarming with 'lawntennysonians'. During the inter-war years there was a second tennis boom that saw new courts provided behind many resort promenades. Bournemouth Corporation was typical in the way that it developed

Crazy golf courses like this one at Bournemouth became popular in the 1960s and have remained a seaside staple ever since.

NORTH BERWICK

Golf became such a popular attraction at the Scottish seaside that holidaymakers went as much for the links as for the beach. In the 1920s, the Prince of Wales made golf and its uniform of plus fours, or baggy tweed knickerbockers, fashionable. (National Railway Museum/Science & Society Picture Library)

recreational spaces, creating its upper and lower pleasure gardens from the 1890s, until it reached a peak of 620 acres available for the public benefit, including thirty-three bowling greens, twenty tennis courts, ten cricket pitches, six football fields, three croquet lawns, two golf courses and two carriage drives.

Golf had a long history in Scotland but there was no English course until 1864, when the Royal North Devon Club was founded beside the sea at Westward Ho! In Scotland, interest increased so dramatically over the period between 1870 and 1914 that holidaymakers quickly came to associate the seaside with both the beach *and* the links. When asked what there was to do at North Berwick one Glaswegian visitor in 1881 answered: 'The reply is easy, and a single word explains it all – golf!' In September 1922 the Prince of Wales (later Duke of Windsor) teed off at St Andrews watched by an audience of thousands. His influence undoubtedly spurred an English mania for the sport and its upper-class uniform of fashionable plus fours, with many seaside resorts shrewdly taking advantage of cheap land prices during the 1920s and 30s to develop their own courses. Seafront putting greens also began to appear at this time and quickly provided a popular pastime for the whole family. When golf became really popular in the 1960s, seafronts were equipped with miniature golf courses, laid out with eighteen obstacle-ridden holes of increasing difficulty. Often labelled 'crazy' golf, its artificial landscape of bridges and windmills remains a familiar image of the seaside.

Other things also went miniature at the seaside. People enjoyed visiting the harbour to watch the boats and many coastal towns had a reputation for sailing. Boating lakes allowed holidaymakers to join in the maritime spirit. As early as 1887 part of the vast stretch of reclaimed land behind Southport beach had been turned into a Marine Lake, where boatmen provided pleasure rides. From the inter-war years,

Boating lakes provided a nice calm arena for holidaymakers to play at being sailors. In the background is Brighton's West Pier complete with fairground and entertainment pavilions.

boating lakes became an expected seaside attraction. At Skegness and Great Yarmouth a network of miniature canals was dug and landscaped, both of these schemes being examples of Depression-era job creation. To make it sound more inviting, the mile-long stretch at Great Yarmouth was dubbed the 'Venetian Waterways' and holidaymakers were free to explore the surrounding gardens with their bridges and lily ponds. In the 1950s and 60s families continued to take to the artificial waters in rowing boats, pedaloes, long-necked swan boats and, behind the seafront at Hunstanton, miniature speed boats powered by outboard motors.

The immediate post-war decades also witnessed the spread of miniature settlements. The first model village opened to the public in 1929 when thousands flocked to see Bekonscot, the 'Real-life Lilliput', created by accountant Roland

This 1950s photograph nicely demonstrates the scale of Ramsgate's Model Village. Similar attractions portraying an idealised England proved popular around the coast in the immediate post-war decades.

Callingham next to his home at Beaconsfield. His idea was subsequently transferred to the seaside and in 1950 the new 'Magic Garden' at Margate's Dreamland included a detailed miniature Tudor village. Three years later it was transferred to Ramsgate's West Cliff, where it became an attraction in its own right. At Southport, Tom Dobbins set about realising his dream to build one of the finest model villages in the country. After opening in his home town in 1956 he found a second site at Babbacombe, near Torquay, where he started to create an idealised vision of the English countryside, peopled by tiny figures and served by a model railway. To advertise South Devon's latest attraction a promotional van was rigged up with a miniature thatched cottage on its roof and the opening hours of 'Miniaturdorf' painted on its side, along with a big reminder to 'Bring your camera'. Model villages were popular with children and as more families were able to visit the seaside in the post-war decades new attractions opened to cater specifically for younger visitors. Peter Pan playgrounds appeared at resorts from Southend to Southport offering roundabouts, slides, swings, go-carts and ices on one colourful seafront site. There were paddling pools for the little ones too, with bright blue floors that turned the shallow water into an exotic aquamarine colour.

The seafront also had a strong commercial element, most conspicuous along flatter stretches of coastline where the landward side of the promenade was a mixture of accommodation and ground-floor business premises. Inter-war cafés and ice cream parlours took their place alongside the existing souvenir sellers and postcard stands. Then there were the fish and chip shops, purveyors of the classic British take-away. Fast rail transport to inland cities meant that by the late nineteenth century fried fish had become a staple food of the working classes. To satisfy their holiday demands, chippies sprang up at every resort serving portions wrapped in newspaper, a packaging that kept the heat in and allowed the steam to soften the food slightly, giving it its distinctive smell, flavour and texture. The tea room, that other great

A kiosk selling ice cream near the harbour at St Ives in Cornwall. A seafront was not complete without plentiful refreshment options.

The 'toast-rack' tram took passengers on a circular tour of Edwardian Blackpool. It cost 6d for a ride and the route included a stop at Whitegate Drive, where a photographer was waiting to take a souvenir snapshot.

Whitegate Drive, Blackpool

British institution, could also be found everywhere along the promenade, in the parks and by the boating lakes and playgrounds.

All these open-air attractions could be quite spread out, so novel forms of transport were invented to carry holidaymakers between them. In 1883 Britain's first electric railway opened in Brighton. The brainchild of Magnus Volk, it ran along the edge of the beach between Madeira Drive and Black Rock. In 1896 Volk unveiled his extraordinary Brighton and Rottingdean Seashore Electric Tramroad, affectionately known as the 'Daddy-long-legs'. Its rails were laid on the inter-tidal zone and the cars were carried on stilts 24 feet above the track. Though it must have been quite an experience to ride above the waves, Volk's sea tram only operated until 1901. Most Edwardian resorts had more conventional trams when these vehicles were in their heyday, whilst at Weston-super-Mare and Blackpool circular sightseeing tours were offered in open-sided 'toast-rack' trams. At some resorts, a bigger problem than getting along the promenade was getting up and down it. In 1873 the Scarborough South Cliff Tramway Company opened Britain's first funicular railway using sea water as a counterweight to operate two cars, the one ascending as the other was descending. The funicular was quickly embraced by other Victorian resorts and across its two bays Scarborough could boast five cliff railways by 1930.

The seaside proved a good testing ground for experimental technology and electricity was quickly taken up in the quest to keep visitors entertained. Along the seafront electric light was used to extend the day and, more importantly, the season. Seaside entrepreneurs covered their buildings in light to entice potential customers and in May 1912 Blackpool put on the first display of what would become its famous illuminations. The 'festoons of garland lamps', made up of some 10,000 light bulbs, were a gesture of welcome to the Royal Family who were visiting the town to open a new section of promenade. Illuminations were suspended during the First World War but began again in Blackpool in 1925. The inter-war period saw many other resorts using electric light to add a romantic yet self-consciously modern

Film and television themes are nothing new at the Blackpool Illuminations. In 1953 the Walt Disney Parade featured favourite cartoon characters on lamp-posts along the promenade. Even the sky is illuminated thanks to a searchlight in the Tower.

flavour to seafront gardens, lidos and amusement parks. Llandudno claimed to be 'very progressive… The Promenade and shelters are illuminated at night by electric light, and are so bright that visitors take their books and evening papers to read while listening to the band.' Southend unveiled its first autumn illuminations in 1935, attracting coach-loads of spectators well into the 1950s. But it was the Blackpool illuminations that went on to become one of the British seaside's great institutions, running each year from late August to early November. Six miles of promenade were transformed into a gallery of electric light, even incorporating public transport as trams and buses were decked out as Mississippi showboats, Cinderella coaches and ocean liners to complement the static set pieces.

Unlike most other outside entertainments, the great advantage of lighting displays was that they were not weather dependent. The British have a well-earned reputation for stoicism in the face of an often damp climate, so it is no surprise that the national pastime of discussing the weather was transferred to the back of postcards. The first picture postcards appeared in 1894, though any message had to be briefly scrawled across the front because the other side was restricted to address only. After 1902 it became legal for the picture to be printed over the entire front with the back now given its familiar division for message to, and address of, the recipient. There was a mania of collecting and sending cards; after comic designs appeared around 1905 trippers joined in so wholeheartedly that the Southend post office could not cope and even opened on Sunday evening, when the waiting crowd stretched across the road. On a card showing the 'Municipal Gardens, Southport, Illuminated', Pollie wrote to Florie back in Sheffield in May 1904: 'We have had the worst weather this time, it has been a gloomy Southport, rain all day yesterday, so we do not look much better for having the week here. Hope you are keeping better and trust that you will have nice weather for your holidays, shall expect to hear from Cleethorpes.' Until holidaymakers could afford to jet off to more guaranteed sunshine they just had to put up with unpredictable British summers. For wet weather days, seaside resorts came up with a range of indoor attractions.

Chapter Nine

PIERS AND PLEASURE PALACES

BY THE END of the 1870s every self-respecting seaside resort had a pier. They were marvels of Victorian engineering that took the seafront promenade and carried it out over the waves. From being purely functional structures, piers developed into places of amusement as vast pavilions were added followed by funfairs and arcades. And as the seaside crowds grew, so did the demand for mass entertainment. At the turn of the century huge indoor leisure complexes sprang up on the seafront, promising enough treats to last from breakfast to bedtime however inclement the weather. Then there were the theatres, spas, winter gardens, Kursaals (from the Germanic word meaning 'cure-hall'), aquariums, hippodromes, cinemas and ballrooms. Holidaymakers could see a different show every night. What they saw changed over time, but the places in which they saw it were always designed to be part of the experience: grand, modern and luxurious palaces for the people.

The first British pier was built in 1814 at Ryde on the Isle of Wight. As paddle steamers began to ply around the coast more wooden landing stages appeared, providing a convenient solution to the problem of passenger disembarkation. Most relied on support from a superstructure of piles driven into the seabed, although the deck of Brighton's 1823 Chain Pier was suspended between cast-iron towers connected by huge chains. There was so much estuary mud to contend with at Southend that its pier of 1830 ultimately became the longest, stretching for a mile and a quarter, nearly twice as long as its nearest competitor for the title at Southport. The latter marked a decisive shift in purpose because it was designed in 1859–60 to act primarily as a promenading pier. Over the first half of the nineteenth century it had become increasingly clear that seaside visitors were walking on the pier for the thrill of it and not just because they had a boat to catch. Piers provided a unique seaside attraction. With this realisation came turnstiles and toll booths, the charges helping to pay for what were very expensive engineering works.

Around the British coastline an average of two new piers were built every year during the 1860s and 70s. Scotland never really took to the pier but by the early twentieth century English and Welsh resorts were self-evidently love-struck: Brighton, Great Yarmouth, Morecambe, Hastings (with St Leonards), Weston-super-Mare and Colwyn Bay (with nearby Rhos-on-Sea) had two apiece. Blackpool reigned supreme with three. From Coatham in the north to Plymouth in the south, from western Aberystwyth to eastern Lowestoft, piers were a seaside phenomenon. Some lasted longer than others. Storms, fires, boat crashes and Second World War security breaches saw off a good few. Post-war neglect also led to a substantial number of demolitions, yet the pier remains a potent seaside symbol into the twenty-first century.

OPPOSITE
Though piers began as functional landing stages they soon became popular as an extension to the promenade. Large entertainment venues were added from the 1870s. This one on Lowestoft's South Pier has the look of a minor country house.

Most piers began as commercial ventures, which needed a steady stream of visitors to achieve a return. Indoor facilities helped provide this. The big innovator was engineer Eugenius Birch, responsible for fourteen piers in England and Wales. In the early 1860s he began to make tentative steps towards integral entertainment buildings, providing Italianate-style kiosks on his Blackpool North Pier and oriental ones on the West Pier at Brighton. In 1869–72 Birch designed a pier for Hastings that included a substantial pavilion. With capacity for 2,000 people, this building also set an important precedent by its fulsome use of oriental design motifs. In 1874 Birch was invited back to Blackpool's North Pier to add a pavilion, this time modelled on the Hindu temple at Binderabund in India. Elsewhere around the coast other styles were also used: the Bournemouth Pier entrance was all spiky Gothic, while Lowestoft's South Pier Pavilion resembled an Arts and Crafts cottage. Yet from the 1890s eastern styles came to the fore, helping to make the Victorian and Edwardian seaside seem excitingly different. Exotic references were used to suggest the enticing fantasy that as holidaymakers walked across the waves they also walked towards the architectural splendour of faraway lands. Morecambe Central Pier got two pavilions in 1897, one of them dubbed the 'Taj Mahal of the North' because of its intricate array of domes, towers, arcades and balconies. Brighton Palace Pier Theatre of 1901 and Southport Pier Pavilion of 1902 were both examples of over-the-top seaside orientalism. Two years later another Lancashire resort, Lytham St Annes, got plentiful onion domes in its handsome Moorish Pavilion.

Marine Palace,
Tea Garden on the roof of the Palace Pier, Brighton

Buildings on the Palace Pier at Brighton exploited the seaside trend for Eastern-inspired architecture. The onion domes look particularly impressive seen at close quarters in the rooftop tea garden.

The entertainment provided in these buildings was a mix of music, theatre and variety. Weston-super-Mare's Grand Pier Pavilion could seat 2,000 and, until its destruction by fire in 1930, offered classic drama seasons, visits from national opera companies and Sunday evening concerts by military bands. Other places presented a distinctive 'end of the pier' show. Morecambe's Indian Theatre became known as

Clacton's 1959 Ocean Revue was a mixture of music and comedy sketches in the best variety tradition. The programme cover for 1959 lists all the other attractions on the pier including amusements and dancing.

CLACTON PIER

ATTRACTIONS

☆ Blue Lagoon
Dancing Daily at 3.30 and 8.00 p.m.
FRIDAY AFTERNOON & SUNDAYS EXCEPTED

☆ Jolly Roger
THEATRE
(COMMENCING JULY)   NIGHTLY AT 8.15 p.m.
(SUNDAYS EXCEPTED)

☆ The Wonder SWIMMING POOL
SWIMMING GALAS — WATER POLO

☆ Rambla CONCERT PARTY
DAILY AT 11 a.m. AND 3 p.m.
(SUNDAYS EXCEPTED)
IF WET, UNDER COVER

CLACTON PIER FOR HEALTHY HAPPINESS

OCEAN THEATRE

MRS. E. KINGSMAN
Presents
THE OCEAN REVUE

Clacton Pier for Healthy Happiness

PROGRAMME · PRICE · THREEPENCE

Pier buildings built after the Second World War were far less elaborate, as can be seen in this example at Bournemouth. When this photograph was taken in the 1960s the end-of-the-pier show was Sing It With Joe. *(John Hinde)*

'The Home of Vaudeville' and, after rebuilding in the wake of a disastrous fire in 1921, Blackpool's North Pier Pavilion became synonymous with Lawrence Wright's variety production *On With the Show*, which ran for thirty years. Alongside singers and comedians, the ranks of chorus girls with long legs and dazzling smiles became a seaside staple. Enduring summer shows in the pier pavilions and seaside theatres of Sussex included the *Fol de Rols*, billed as 'the show for high brows, low brows and no brows', and *Twinkle* produced by Clarkson Rose with his wife and co-star Olive Fox. Beginning in the 1930s, these revues offered cleverer material than seaside audiences had been used to with Pierrots and concert parties as well as the excitement of more lavish productions. They remained popular at resorts like Eastbourne, Bognor Regis and Worthing for forty years. By the 1950s and 60s there was also a move back towards a Victorian entertainment format now called 'Old Tyme Music Hall', often with the inclusion of well-known celebrity performers. From the outset, stars of radio and cinema proved a big lure for seaside audiences and many young actors and comedians appeared in summer shows before going on to high-profile television careers. Indeed, as TV grew in popularity, stage versions of favourite programmes became a feature of seaside entertainment and as the summer revues began to disappear in the 1960s, comedy took over at the end of the pier. Big name comedians like Norman Wisdom, Tommy Cooper, Tony Hancock, Morecambe and Wise, Larry Grayson and Ken Dodd were seaside regulars.

In one form or another, theatrical entertainments proved their worth at the seaside. Aquariums, offering a more educational type of show, with clear coastal associations, proved distinctly less popular. Two of them, at Brighton (1872) and

Scarborough (1877), were designed by pier engineer Eugenius Birch. Both were built underground, around a series of huge sea water tanks that visitors could look into from a network of corridors, classically styled at Brighton and oriental at Scarborough. Both faced closure by the 1920s. Brighton Council took over the Sussex site and the aquarium that they rebuilt is still in operation. In Yorkshire, attempts to woo visitors included transforming the aquarium into a swimming pool, a theatre, a skating rink and a zoo. After purchase by the corporation it re-opened in 1925 as Galaland with slot machines, fairground rides and musical concerts alongside the remaining fish tanks. In 1968 it was demolished and turned into a car park.

A number of aquariums were built around the coast during the 1870s but most proved too big to be financially viable. As this picture shows, the Aquarium and Winter Garden at Tynemouth dominated Long Sands beach.

Great Yarmouth Aquarium was projected to be a seafront landmark, but the money had already run out by the time it opened in 1876. Though the over-ambitious winter garden was shelved the building could still boast eighteen fish tanks and ponds for crocodiles and alligators, a roof-top roller skating rink (these were easy to provide and satisfied a craze that came back again in the 1900s, 1930s and 1950s), a dining room, reading room and open air theatre. A disappointed visitor in 1877 noted that 'Natural History seems to take second place to the concert room and the restaurant'. By 1881 the aquarium company was bankrupt. Having learnt a valuable lesson, the new owners reopened as the Royal Aquarium Theatre showing musical comedy, thrillers and variety, with a rebuilt banqueting hall that could seat 1,000. The original architects of Great Yarmouth Aquarium also designed a huge brick-faced aquarium and winter garden at Tynemouth, but the business failed there just as rapidly. From 1903–27 it became the Tynemouth Music Hall, then from 1933 the Tynemouth Plaza theatre and ballroom.

The Blackpool Tower complex opened in 1894 offering multiple entertainments under one roof. Five years later The Alhambra opened next door, but whereas the Tower was a great success, it was not.

Blackpool Winter Gardens opened in 1878. By the end of the century it was actively competing against the new Blackpool Tower attractions, adding the Empress Ballroom and adjacent Indian Lounge in 1896.

What the aquarium example makes clear is that, however grand the building, seaside holidaymakers would only patronise a venue if they liked what was on offer inside. There *were* successful entertainment complexes on a large scale but profits were not guaranteed, not even at Blackpool. Visitor numbers were rising so fast by the 1890s that Lancashire's favourite resort could afford to make a statement.

Great Yarmouth Winter Gardens is the last example built of iron and glass to survive. During the 1960s it was converted to a German Biergarten *complete with mountain scenery.*

On Whit Monday 1894 Blackpool Tower opened, the ultimate advertisement for attractions gathered together on an entirely new scale. The complex which bore its name boasted an aquarium, menagerie, circus, Grand Pavilion (later converted to the famous Tower Ballroom), multiple shops, cafes and bars as well as the unique lift ride to the crow's nest of the tower itself. In order to compete with this array of delights, the nearby Winter Garden responded by adding the Empress Ballroom to attractions which already included a theatre encircled by glazed promenades and an opera house; fierce rivalry between the two kept entertainments fresh at both well into the twentieth century. But there was a limit and The Alhambra of 1899 exceeded it. Next to the tower complex, in one massive seafront building, speculators hoped to fill a 2,000-seat circus, a ballroom for 3,000 dancers and a 3,000-seat theatre. In view of all the other venues already in existence it was hardly surprising that by 1902 The Alhambra was unable to pay its running costs. It was incorporated into the Tower and operated as the Palace until demolition in 1961.

Away from Blackpool, the spending power of Lancashire trippers was also driving the creation of major mass entertainment venues at New Brighton and Rhyl. The former showed itself to have serious pretensions when construction of a tower to beat Blackpool's began in 1897. All of these palatial complexes were designed to elicit superlatives, but the reality of making the largest theatre in the country outside London pay for itself got the better of shareholders at New Brighton. The tower was demolished in 1919–21; the remaining buildings, originally including a ballroom for 2,000 couples and a winter garden, were destroyed in a fire of 1969. At Rhyl, the great glass dome of the Queen's Palace was a seafront fixture of sadly short duration, lasting just five years before the ballroom and the mock-up of Venice below it (complete with real canals and gondolas), the theatre, winter garden, zoo, waxworks and forty shops, also went up in smoke. For the average working man and woman these indoor facilities represented a wonderland of undreamt luxury that they enjoyed during their brief seaside visit. Many thousands walked through the doors but the scale of these buildings rapidly turned them into white elephants.

Elsewhere in the country a holidaymaker's entertainment needs were more likely to be catered for by a number of independent venues, including the pier pavilion. Circus shows were provided in permanent hippodromes as well as under the big tops of travelling showmen. Winter gardens began as a place to demonstrate the wonders of Victorian horticulture, a good wet weather option at the seaside because of their ability to bring the outdoors in. The obvious precedent was London's vast Crystal Palace, which was moved to a permanent site at Sydenham after the Great Exhibition of 1851. Eastbourne got its iron and glass winter garden in 1874 and when Southport Winter Garden opened in the same year it claimed to be the 'largest conservatory in England'. The glasshouse took up half of a building that also featured a concert hall with an audience capacity of 2,500. Predictably enough it suffered financial difficulties, just like the Bournemouth Winter Garden of 1876. The Torquay example built in 1878–81 had a miserable start but enjoyed greater success after it was taken to pieces and shipped around the coast to Great Yarmouth. It opened on the east coast in 1904 and went through numerous different uses including concert hall, indoor roller skating rink and 1960s *Biergarten*. Musical entertainment was the mainstay of this type of venue, also the case for the Kursaals that made a brief appearance at Bexhill-on-Sea and Weymouth around the turn of the century. The Germanic name was used to describe public rooms at Continental spa resorts but in Britain was simply applied for novelty value.

Winter gardens continued to be built in the early twentieth century, though by this time the name had become divorced from any expectation of plant displays.

Though the German word 'Kursaal' translates as 'cure-hall', the few English buildings to take the name were purely for entertainment. Weymouth Kursaal was built as a concert venue in 1905.

The De La Warr Pavilion at Bexhill-on-Sea was designed by Russian architect Serge Chermayeff and his German partner Erich Mendelsohn. It was originally intended to form part of a bigger development of hotels, apartments and shops.

The Margate Winter Garden of 1911 was built into the cliff top at Cliftonville. At Rothesay the circular domed structure of 1923 was prefabricated to provide covered seating around a pre-existing bandstand. The striking Modernist Winter Garden at Ventnor on the Isle of Wight (1935) had a glass-fronted tower, but it was designed as a sun-trap for humans not exotic flora. The most iconic seaside building of the inter-war years was undoubtedly the De La Warr Pavilion at Bexhill-on-Sea. Internationally stylish, it put the quiet Sussex seaside town on the map, offering a spacious up-to-date interior with large theatre, restaurant, library, conference room and lounge, plus outside terraces for sun bathing and a rooftop sundeck where visitors could play quoits and other games popular on ocean liners. Scarborough, Whitby and Bridlington called their main entertainment buildings 'The Spa', in the former case for very good reason since it was built on the site of the original mineral spring that made Scarborough famous. The Spa was considered the smartest of Scarborough's music venues and although people could still drink the health-giving waters, by the post-war period they were more likely to go and listen to Max Jaffa, whose orchestral concerts from the Palm Court were frequently broadcast on BBC Radio in the 1950s and 60s.

During the 1950s and 60s Max Jaffa was a much-loved fixture at Scarborough, playing regular concerts with the Spa Orchestra, many of which were broadcast by the BBC.

To stay ahead of the game, seaside resorts had to adopt the latest forms of entertainment. From the early twentieth century this meant that live performances had new competition from the big screen. Numerous attempts were made to develop moving pictures and the seaside offered willing audiences for experimental technology. Within weeks of the first films being shown in London in 1896, the Pandora Gallery at Brighton brought cinema to the seaside. Early films could be shown in any darkened hall but purpose-built venues began to appear in the Edwardian period. The oldest surviving seaside example is at Great Yarmouth, where The Gem opened for

Seventy years after Great Yarmouth Hippodrome opened in 1903, the show featured acrobats, elephants and Bulgarian Artistes from 'behind the Iron Curtain'. Like the Blackpool Tower Circus it has a ring that can be filled with water.

cinematograph showings in 1908. In the first four days 17,000 people paid to see what was billed as 'a continuous flow of Electric Vaudeville'. Soon every resort had at least one cinema. As the Hollywood influence grew, cinema design took on the striking forms of Art Deco and audiences could not seem to get enough of the movies. During the 1930s Brighton and Bournemouth could each boast sixteen cinemas, while Blackpool had nineteen. This was the peak of their dominance and closures began after the Second World War as television began to take over. A new use was found for some cinema buildings thanks to bingo, another influential American import that grew increasingly popular in the 1960s. The game took

America by storm in the 1930s and 40s, crossing the Atlantic after the war where it proved popular in seafront amusement arcades. Calls like 'legs eleven' and 'eighty-eight two fat ladies' also helped give it a hint of saucy seaside humour.

By the second half of the twentieth century, ballrooms and dance halls were also seeking new uses. Dancing was a sociable activity that had been well established as a seaside diversion since Georgian visitors were provided with assembly rooms. All the big Victorian leisure complexes included grand ballrooms where couples could whirl in a majestic setting. They were no less popular during the inter-war years, though by the 1930s there was a greater informality to the ritual of dancing, drinking and picking up members of the opposite sex. There were ballrooms at holiday camps and large hotels while dancing on the pier was another option, either in the open air or in new dance halls. The very name of Clacton pier's Blue Lagoon Dance Hall captured the essence of the glass and chrome era. But by the 1950s ballroom and tea dances were considered entertainment for the older generation. Pop music was creating new dance styles. Jiving and jitterbugging were disallowed in the ballroom at Southend Kursaal because the impact on the sprung floor caused the mirror ball to swing alarmingly and the whole building to vibrate. In the 1960s live bands began to be replaced by jukeboxes and when the big name performers came to the seaside it was more likely to be on tour than for a summer season. The Beatles, the Rolling Stones, the Hollies and the Kinks all played seaside venues that were built for theatre and variety. From the 1870s to the 1970s the seaside catered for every new craze, but because entertainment was such a large part of the seaside economy the impact of changes in taste was magnified by the sheer number of venues.

Dancing was a popular seaside activity in the early twentieth century. The shape of this ballroom was determined by the eight legs of New Brighton's short-lived tower, under which it was built.

Chapter Ten

THE LATEST AMUSEMENTS

Seaside attractions were ever-changing because their appeal relied on novelty. Holidaymakers wanted to be amused, entertained, excited and even a little frightened, so vast pleasure beaches sprang up to offer the most thrilling rides and the newest sensations. Though their roots lay in travelling fairs, permanent amusement parks could afford to invest in bigger and better equipment. They were monuments to cheap power and light; electricity and technology fused for the delight of seaside crowds. America led the way in commercial leisure, exerting a huge influence on British amusement parks as popular culture became enthralled by the latest import from across the Atlantic. Some rides arrived at the seaside by way of international exhibitions, the testing ground for new inventions that gave them an unassailable pedigree; 'direct from Earl's Court' was a popular boast in the early twentieth century. Then there were the sideshows and slot machines, gathered together on piers and in seafront amusement arcades. The relaxed atmosphere of the seaside allowed adults to indulge their childish side. It made them freer with their pennies, willing to gamble on the chance of winning a prize and happy to spend money on stomach-churning rides that elsewhere might seem pointless.

By the late nineteenth century, seaside visitors had already been introduced to the switchback railway and the mutoscope, precursors of modern roller coasters and arcade games. For the price of one penny, holidaymakers could turn the mutoscope handle to flip pictures that created an illusion of movement, giving a window into the voyeuristic world of 'what the butler saw'. Proving that the taste for sex and suspense is nothing new, these early slot machines titillated with scenes of mild striptease and racy titles like 'Parisian Can-Can', 'The Naked Truth' and 'Death Dive'. They were soon to be found on every pier in the country. Other penny machines joined them and their growing popularity led to the creation of amusement halls. One of the earliest was the Jubilee Exhibition at Great Yarmouth, burnt down in 1901 but rebuilt as The Paradium. It was run by the Barrons, a family who had links to the fairground world as well as being entertainment managers and slot machine manufacturers. The Edwardian appetite for slot machines was fed by inventive new machines that included the 'New Auto Piano', in which lay the origins of the jukebox, and 'The Elk', on which the player had to line up spinning coloured bands in the first example of what would later become the ubiquitous fruit machine.

During the inter-war years slot machines spread through practically every seaside town. In the 1920s 'Fun City' came to Bridlington's North Marine Drive, Clacton Pier had the 'Crystal Casino Amusement Arcade' and at Brighton the Palace Pier Theatre was converted into the 'Palace of Fun', offering a ripe selection of circus

OPPOSITE
Although Porthcawl's Coney Beach took its name from Coney Island, the American home of amusement arcades, there was always room for traditional British fairground rides like the carousel or 'Gallopers'. (National Railway Museum/Science & Society Picture Library)

OPPOSITE
Amusement arcades first appeared at the seaside in the Edwardian period. Inside, the mechanical devices eventually gave way to electronic Space Invaders, and the fairground organ music to piped pop 'muzak'.

BELOW
Mutoscopes, otherwise known as 'what the butler saw' machines, were found on piers around the country. The titles absorbing these boys include 'Easy Street' and 'Dance of Love'. (National Railway Museum/Science & Society Picture Library)

acts, waxworks, shooting galleries and penny machines. The very word 'fun' seemed to be imbued with tempting new commercial meanings. By 1939 arcades were filled with a mix of traditional machines and newer electrical devices. Fortune telling, an old seaside favourite, was now possible without human intervention thanks to a plethora of card-spewing contraptions whose names took advantage of exciting technological advances. Among those available at Blackpool were the 'Green Ray Television Wonder', 'The Robot King', 'The Radio Analyst' and 'The Electrical Crystal Gazer'. In the myriad amusement centres and along Blackpool's Golden Mile, the most common slot machine was the 'Football Game' where two players competed; other variations included hockey, polo and golf games. A popular import from Germany was the 'Clucking Hen', a machine that delivered coloured metal eggs filled with 'swag'. Until Hitler switched the manufacturers on to more serious products, five million eggs were being supplied to British arcades every year. By the 1960s arcades were dominated by electronic games and machines in which enticing piles of pennies sat waiting for one more coin to push them over the edge, down the chute and into the holidaymakers' waiting hands.

The amusements business was always quick to respond to developments in popular culture, but in the large parks it also sought to create an environment that took people away from the outside world. Coney Island, the New Yorker's resort of choice on the

These 1930s holidaymakers are standing in front of the Rainbow Wheel at Blackpool Pleasure Beach. A popular ride since 1912, it offered a sequence of views and sensations while the customer remained almost static.

eastern seaboard of America, provided important lessons in how to achieve this fantasy vision. Three amusement parks were created there in the years after 1897 called Steeplechase, Luna Park and Dreamland. Their very names were calculated to appeal and by virtue of association they would later lend glamour to British ventures. Everything at Coney Island was designed to impress, from the extreme amusements and mechanical rides to the exotic sideshows and freakish displays of humanity. The goal there, as in all the amusement parks that followed, was to restore adults to their childish capacity for wonder through an assault on the senses; in close proximity there were rides that flung people around, hurled them into space, plunged them down into water and lured them along dark passages into the fascinating or frightening unknown. Nowhere were people more ready for this transformation than at the seaside.

Blackpool Pleasure Beach was by far the most successful of its kind and is still going strong, with more than six million visitors a year at the beginning of the twenty-first century. Among the South Shore sand dunes, close to the sea and on the edge of the resort, the core elements of a funfair grew around a long-established gypsy encampment. At the end of the electric tram route, it was easily accessible to Blackpool holidaymakers but marginal enough to provide plenty of cheap land for the new generation of rides. The Pleasure Beach gained its name in 1905 after which time it grew rapidly under the guiding hand of William George Bean, a Londoner who had spent time in America during his youth and worked in the Philadelphia amusement machinery industry. He returned to Britain in the mid-1890s and eventually settled in Blackpool with the intention of creating an American-style amusement park. In 1904 Hiram Maxim leased a site at Blackpool for his 'Captive Flying Machine', a by-product of his attempts at aeroplane design in which cars 'flew' at high speed around a central driving shaft. Over the next five years other attractions from the US arrived, several via international exhibitions, and by 1909 Blackpool Pleasure Beach was the largest, most modern amusement park in the country. Its permanence was reinforced in 1913 by a new entrance building called the Casino, an exotic fantasy of architectural borrowings that housed a 700-seat cinema, billiards room and restaurant. In the 1930s the Casino was rebuilt as part of a major modernisation programme that demonstrated Blackpool Pleasure Beach was committed to staying at the cutting edge. Symptomatic of this was the 1950s conversion of cars on the Captive Flying Machine from aeroplanes into space age rockets. Both Bean and his son-in-law successor, Leonard Thompson, made regular trips across the Atlantic to keep abreast of the latest ideas, but they also maintained and updated the best-loved rides; combined with a strong family management it was this that ensured the crowds kept coming.

At Margate the seafront amusement park grew from a venue called 'The Hall by the Sea', converted from a disused railway terminal into an entertainment centre during the 1860s. Victorian showman 'Lord' George Sanger oversaw refurbishment in 1874 and with a keen appreciation of the mass market turned the business into a success, bringing music hall performers down from London and keeping the bar open all day. He created pleasure gardens on the derelict railway sidings and in the 1890s the old buildings were superseded by a purpose-built complex. In 1919, the site was purchased by John Henry Iles, who had decided to become an amusement park entrepreneur after seeing the profitability of North American theme parks whilst touring with a brass band in 1906. Iles brought the 'Scenic Railway' back to England and subsequently went on to own amusement parks around the world, naming them all after the famous pioneers at Coney Island. When Margate re-opened under his management in 1920 it had been transformed into Dreamland. At its centre was a scenic railway that was nearly a mile long. Other favourite rides were added, the massive ballroom was converted into a cinema and the old bar became a cocktail lounge. During the eighteen years of his ownership Iles spent more than £500,000, a fair proportion of which went on the modernisation of the seafront entrance with its distinctive Art Deco fin. In the post-war period new attractions were added and business boomed. The reinventions and investment

From the 1930s, Dreamland's seafront entrance had a distinctive Art Deco fin that acted as a huge signpost to Margate's amusement park. The entrance building originally housed the Sunshine Café with panoramic sea views, an air-conditioned cinema and maple-floored ballroom.

Southend Kursaal was planned as an entertainments complex on the model of Blackpool Tower. During the 1920s a large amusement park was developed on the land behind the main building.

continued but the allure of Margate had waned by the end of the twentieth century, when it was hard to see anything but irony in the once hopeful name of Dreamland.

Southend Kursaal followed a similar trajectory. Inspired by the Blackpool Tower complex, it opened in July 1901 with a circus, ballroom, menagerie and an arcade of shops decorated to look like a street in Cairo featuring shooting galleries and all 'the latest Yankee notions'. Two years later it was up for sale. The Luna Park Company took over with plans for new attractions and rides including an American bowling alley. After all these attempts at importing ideas from the United States, it was fitting that the park's real saviour came in the shape of Clifton Jay Morehouse, the American inventor of the gas radiator. He and his son ran the Kursaal Gardens as an amusement park, expanding throughout the 1920s until the post-war peak in the 1950s and 60s when the 700-space coach park was often full to capacity. It closed in 1973 but was partially re-opened in 1998.

Of all the rides on offer, roller coasters dominated amusement parks with their size and speedy thrills. Their genealogy is contested but a flurry of American patents in the 1870s and 80s suggest that by then the roller coaster's time had come. 'Thompson's Gravity Switchback' was a low-technology version that began to appear on the British coast from the 1880s. Holidaymakers rode in open cars on a wooden track, travelling through a series of dips to the end of the outward track where a switch transferred them onto a second parallel track for the return journey. The 500-foot-long Great Yarmouth switchback opened in 1887 and proved such a novelty that its takings on August Bank Holiday Monday more than covered the season's ground rent of £100. Circuits were the next step and the first to appear at Blackpool was the *Montagnes Russes* or 'Russian Mountains' which came from Paris

Figure Eight, Skegness

and was erected in the grounds of the Winter Garden in 1902. Five years later John Henry Iles gave Blackpool Pleasure Beach its first wooden roller coaster in the form of a 40-foot-high scenic railway on which passengers travelled at 35 miles per hour, faster than most motor cars of the period. Views from literature and legend provided the scenic content. In 1920 the 'Big Dipper' was introduced at a New Jersey amusement park, the first to make use of new under-track friction wheels and rollers. William George Bean bought the UK rights and introduced Blackpool to a

The popular appeal of roller coasters meant that they were built on beaches as well as in dedicated amusement parks. In 1910 the 'Figure Eight' was a big attraction at Skegness.

Smiles and screams on the roller coaster at Southport Pleasureland. This park was run by the Thompson family of Blackpool Pleasure Beach.

The Water Chute was a favourite ride at seaside amusement parks, seen here in the Pleasure Gardens at Whitley Bay. A sign at the top warned passengers to keep their arms and legs in the car.

Water Chute
Pleasure Gardens Spanish City, Whitley Bay.

ride with faster speeds, tighter curves and steeper drops. With each new reinvention of the roller coaster Blackpool Pleasure Beach led the way, ending the 1970s with a sign of adventures to come. In 1979 'Revolution' was the first steel-looping coaster in Britain and the first £1 million ride.

Amusement parks needed a variety of different rides to thrive and an added watery element proved very popular when tested around the turn of the twentieth century. From Weston-super-Mare to Whitley Bay crowds queued to descend the 'Water Chute'. Patrons boarded boats at the top of a high tower from where they were released down a steep incline, hitting the large pool below with a mighty splash. Once the soggy passengers had disembarked, the boats were hauled back up the incline on a chain ready to start again. In the 1930s this idea was integrated into the circuits of wooden roller coasters at Porthcawl, Blackpool and Southend. It was a logical step from there to the 'Log Flume', a new ride introduced at Blackpool Pleasure Beach in 1966; seated in 'logs', passengers were swept along a channelled flow of water through a series of tunnels, raises and drops. Another precedent for this ride was the Edwardian 'River Caves', which were to the 'Log Flume' what the 'Scenic Railway' was to the roller coaster. This water ride through a series of brightly coloured caves found success at Coney Island in 1904, transferring to Blackpool via Earl's Court within the year. A version purchased for Margate's Dreamland was colloquially known as 'The Tubs' because passengers glided along a swift flowing waterway in huge metal bins. It was aimed at families but the dark seclusion of the ride's progress through a series of plaster and cement backdrops, including the Ice Cave, Smugglers' Cave and Venetian Cave, also appealed to courting couples.

The frisson of contact between the sexes played an important part in rides that actively disorientated participants. Dishevelment was always an outcome of riding the 'Joy Wheel'. It arrived at Blackpool Pleasure Beach from Coney Island in 1910, quickly earning its name as female legs and undergarments were exposed as a result

The 'Joy Wheel' was notorious for throwing people into dizzy disarray and the ladies in this cartoon are clearly too refined to go on a ride that would undoubtedly reveal more than an ankle.

of the disarray it caused. The Hastings example was housed in a circular building at the shore end of the pier where spectators could watch holidaymakers try to stay seated on the spinning wheel. According to a local newspaper report, 'it revolves at a giddy speed and hurls its victim yards along the glazed floor'. A variation of this ride, called the 'Social Mixer', later appeared in Blackpool's 'Fun House'; one observer described how the dizzying speeds in the large spinning bowl caused minor orgies and violent sickness! With its moving floors the Modernist 'Fun House' was an updated version of the perennial favourite 'Noah's Ark'. Another American innovation, this huge model boat began rocking atop an artificial Mount Ararat in 1922. Each step on the way through the Ark was liable to bring a new surprise as the floor shook, sank, rocked and rotated. One visitor in 1938 remarked how the

'Noah's Ark' proved a huge hit at Blackpool Pleasure Beach. The base of Mount Ararat was full of model animals in such bizarre pairings as an elephant with a rabbit on its back and a polar bear with a foxhound. Hiram Maxim's 'Flying Machine' is to the left and the 'Rainbow Wheel' to the right.

A publicity shot of the Brooklands Racers taken in 1949 as Dreamland entered its post-war boom years. (Bill Evans Collection)

OPPOSITE BOTTOM
The Revolving Tower at Great Yarmouth was a seafront feature from 1897 to 1941. The car, capable of carrying 150 passengers, revolved around steel columns and was powered by a steam engine that operated wire ropes and weights.

'whole ship pitches constantly in a very realistic way' further noting that most parties who went through 'clung together screaming in the dark'.

Clustered around the big rides were other favourites like the carousel, 'Dodgems', 'Helter Skelter', 'Ghost Train' and 'Waltzers'. Then there were the shooting galleries and sideshows that brought all the fun of the fairground to seaside amusement parks. Frenchman Arsene Jules Lecorgne was a travelling showman who had exhibitions at coastal resorts including Colwyn Bay, New Brighton and Cleethorpes. He and his family settled at Southend where they ran stalls at the Kursaal from 1902. Among these were Hoop La and coconut shies, 'Sweets Aux Champagne' and 'Dandies', a game that required a good aim to knock the top hats off smartly dressed mannequins moving around on a turntable as if they were taking a stroll in St James' Park. Other sideshows featured real people, like 'Tip 'Em Out of Bed', in which a scantily clad girl was plunged into the water every time a ball hit the target above her bed, and the 'Wall of Death'. From the 1930s awe-struck visitors to the Kursaal looked on as George 'Tornado' Smith rode his motorbike around a sheer-sided drum while performing such tricks as standing in the saddle, riding backwards and doing handstands on the handlebars. Sensational displays were also shipped in, including Al Capone's car shown at the Kursaal and the vehicles used in the Great Train Robbery put on view at Dreamland.

One final type of amusement is worth mentioning because it gave holidaymakers an opportunity to survey the entire seaside scene. After Blackpool's successful attempt to rival the Eiffel Tower, plans were made for a variety of different towers around the coast. Similar-looking structures sought to go higher than Blackpool's 500 feet; foundations were laid for a 530-foot tower at Southend Kursaal and the New Brighton Tower was actually built to a height of 576 feet. Morecambe's 1889 tower was a less ambitious conical design reaching 252 feet. In order to offer views from its existing site, Blackpool Winter Gardens bought the 220-foot-high Gigantic Wheel in 1896, which offered a leisurely ride in thirty carriages, each with capacity for thirty people. It was never as popular as the Blackpool Tower and was demolished in 1929. None of the imitators proved as long-lasting as the original, but as a variation on the theme, revolving towers also enjoyed a brief moment of popularity in the 1890s. Invented in America, the first British revolving tower was built at Great Yarmouth in 1897 followed by others at Southend and Cleethorpes. Proving that towers had continuing appeal, a plan was revealed in 1964 to provide Brighton seafront with a £1 million 'Skydeck'. It was to be 1,000 feet high, built at the end of a 300-foot pier, with a restaurant, observation decks and even a type of high-rise aquarium. Billed as 'outrageously modern', it was never built. At the beginning of the twenty-first century, however, work is due to begin on a similar tower called 'i-360', designed to replace Brighton's lost West Pier with a vertical monument. Recreated for different generations, the seaside thrills of dizzying heights and high-speed rides have always found an audience and will continue to do so.

ABOVE
It looks like Blackpool Tower but it was actually 70 feet taller. New Brighton Tower offered spectacular views but it only lasted twenty years before it was demolished.

Chapter Eleven

THE FUTURE OF THE SEASIDE HOLIDAY

T HIS BOOK looks at the heyday of the British seaside holiday and for that reason it does not go beyond the 1970s. By that point competition from foreign resorts had already begun to have a huge effect on holiday habits, as more and more people could afford to fly off to hotter climes. Statistical evidence proves that British resorts continued to welcome millions of visitors in the last quarter of the twentieth century but, even if the death of the British seaside is a myth, the fact remains that by the 1980s and 90s it had become deeply unfashionable. The seaside always relied on novelty but after the Second World War it lost its edge. Investment in new attractions was minimal. Towns that had once been the heartland of everything new and exciting began to look increasingly shabby. Today's nostalgic vision of the traditional bucket and spade holiday follows a period of rejection when the old-fashioned seaside was just that: out-of-date, expensive and not sunny enough.

In the first decade of the twenty-first century, however, there are real signs of a renewed interest in the seaside as a holiday destination. After several decades of exploring the wider world, British people are rediscovering the amazingly varied coastline on their own doorstep. And by relying on their unique selling points many

Buckets and spades are still strongly associated with British seaside holidays. These brightly coloured examples were for sale at Great Yarmouth in 2008.

smaller seaside resorts have carved out a successful niche. These include places like Southwold in Suffolk, famous for its beach huts and old-world charm, Whitstable in Kent with its oyster festival, and St Ives in Cornwall, with its Tate gallery and beautiful beaches. Art and culture have found fertile ground on the British coast often with government funded regeneration projects. Weekend breaks offer opportunities for year-round tourism if seaside resorts can offer what a new generation of discerning visitors is looking for, good food, culture and heritage as well as old-fashioned nostalgia. The sexy, raucous seaside is alive and well in Blackpool's stag and hen parties, but the first working-class seaside resort is also seeking World Heritage Site status for its contribution to Britain's popular culture. The challenge for all seaside resorts is to capitalise on what makes them distinctive. The Victorians and Edwardians used fanciful architecture to make the seaside feel like a different place, but buildings from the post-Second World War decades rarely showed any recognition of their special location on the coast. That is also beginning to change. Inventiveness is returning to the seaside. Boscombe will be home to Europe's first artificial surf reef and its neglected 1950s beach huts have had a designer revamp. Environmental considerations are beginning to affect the decisions people make about their holiday destinations, so if resorts can keep the best of the past and create new facilities that look good and that people want to use, there is real hope for another golden era of British seaside holidays. And the piers, the donkeys, the buckets and spades, the sticky rock and the illuminations will be part of that too.

On a hot sunny day British people still gravitate towards the seaside. In August 2002 holidaymakers were doing the same things on Weymouth beach as generations had done before them.

FURTHER READING

Akhtar, Miriam, and Humphries, Steve. *Some Liked it Hot: The British on Holiday at Home and Abroad*. Virgin Publishing, 2000.

Anderson, Janice, and Swinglehurst, Edmund. *The Victorian and Edwardian Seaside*, second edition. Bounty Books, 2005.

Braggs, Steven, and Harris, Diane. *Sun, Fun and Crowds: Seaside Holidays Between the Wars*. Tempus Publishing, 2000.

Brodie, Allan, and Winter, Gary. *England's Seaside Resorts*. English Heritage, 2007.

Durie, Alistair J. *Scotland for the Holidays: Tourism in Scotland c. 1780–1939*. Tuckwell Press, 2003.

Evans, Nick. *Dreamland Remembered: 140 Years of Seaside Fun in Margate*. Privately published, 2003.

Everritt, Sylvia. *Southend Seaside Holiday*. Phillimore, 1980.

Ferry, Kathryn. *Beach Huts and Bathing Machines*. Shire Publications, 2009.

Ferry, Kathryn. *Sheds on the Seashore: A Tour through Beach Hut History*. Indepenpress, 2009.

Gray, Fred. *Designing the Seaside: Architecture, Society and Nature*. Reaktion, 2006.

Hannavy, John. *The English Seaside in Victorian and Edwardian Times*. Shire Publications, 2003.

Hudson, John. *Wakes Week: Memories of Mill Town Holidays*. Alan Sutton, 1992.

Johnson, W. H. *Seaside Entertainment in Sussex*. S. B. Publications, 2001.

Lansdell, Avril. *Seaside Fashions 1860–1939: A Study of Clothes Worn In or Beside the Sea*. Shire Publications, 1990.

Lindley, Kenneth. *Seaside Architecture*. Hugh Evelyn, 1973.

Lenček, Lena, and Bosker, Gideon. *The Beach: The History of Paradise on Earth*. Pimlico, 1999.

Pearson, Lynn F. *Piers and Other Seaside Architecture*. Shire Publications, 2002.

Pertwee, Bill. *Beside the Seaside: A Celebration of 100 Years of Seaside Entertainment*. Collins & Brown, 1999.

Walton, John K. *The English Seaside Resort: A Social History, 1870–1914*. Leicester University Press, 1983.

Walton, John K. *The British Seaside: Holidays and Resorts in the Twentieth Century*. Manchester University Press, 2000.

Walton, John K. *Riding on Rainbows: Blackpool Pleasure Beach and its Place in British Popular Culture*. Skelter Publishing, 2007.

Walvin, James. *Beside the Seaside*. Allen Lane, 1978.

Ward, Colin, and Hardy, Dennis. *Goodnight Campers! The History of the British Holiday Camp*. Mansell Publishing Ltd, 1986.

PLACES TO VISIT

Beside the Seaside Museum, 32 Queen Street, Bridlington, East Yorkshire, YO15 2SP.
   Telephone: 01262 608890.
   Website: www.bridlington.net
Blackpool Tower, Promenade, Blackpool, Lancashire, FY1 4BJ.
   Telephone: 01253 622242.
   Website: www.theblackpooltower.co.uk
Herne Bay Museum and Gallery, 12 William Street, Herne Bay, Kent, CT6 5EJ.
   Telephone: 01227 367368.
   Website: www.canterbury.gov.uk
Margate Museum, The Old Town Hall, Market Place, Margate, CT9 1ER
   Telephone: 01843 231213.
   Website: www.margatemuseum.org.uk
North Somerset Museum, Burlington Street, Weston-super-Mare, Somerset,
   BS23 1PR.
   Telephone: 01934 621028.
   Website: www.n-somerset.gov.uk
Southend-on-Sea Pier Museum, Marine Parade, Southend-on-Sea, Essex, SS1 1EE.
   Telephone: 01702 611214.
   Website: www.southendpiermuseum.co.uk
Time and Tide: Museum of Great Yarmouth Life, Blackfriars Road, Great
   Yarmouth, Norfolk, NR30 3BX.
   Telephone: 01493 743930.
   Website: www.museums.norfolk.gov.uk
Weymouth Museum, Brewers Quay, Hope Square, Weymouth, Dorset, DT4 8TR.
   Telephone: 01305 777622.
   Website: www.weymouthmuseum.org.uk

WEBSITES

www.seasidehistory.co.uk
www.thesurfingmuseum.co.uk
www.butlinsmemories.com

INDEX

Page numbers in italics refer to illustrations